The Cultural Downgrade and the Path to Renewal

Written by Virgil A. Walker

Published by House Walker Publishing

Introduction: The Cultural Downgrade and the Pop Culture Threat

Imagine a garden, not the pristine Eden of old, but one we've tended, where once thrived the sturdy blooms of tale and song, now strangled by a creeping weed: the glowing screen. In this year 2026, our children, bright, curious souls, struggle to read simple words, with four in ten, as the National Assessment of Educational Progress reveals, falling below basic literacy. Why? Their eyes, for seven hours daily, are glued not to the pages of Homer's epics or the hearthside tales of our kin, but to a ceaseless stream of images spun by algorithms that prize profit over truth or beauty. We've traded the ancient schoolroom, where virtue and wisdom were cultivated, for a factory of utility, sowing compliance where discernment once grew. This is no mere change in taste; it is a wounding of the human soul, a step toward what C.S. Lewis called the abolition of man.

The Withering of Minds

This decay is starkest in our schools. According to the 2024 National Assessment of Educational Progress (NAEP), 40% of fourth graders performed below the NAEP Basic level in reading—the highest percentage since 2002—meaning they struggle with fundamental reading skills needed for simple texts. This is up from 37% in 2022 and reflects ongoing post-pandemic challenges, with only 31% of fourth graders performing at or above NAEP Proficient (down 2 percentage points from 2022).

Many students also face difficulties in mathematics: for eighth graders, 39% performed below NAEP Basic in 2024 (up 1 percentage point from 2022), while fourth-grade math showed slight improvement with 39% at or above Proficient (up 3 percentage points from 2022). Once, our schoolrooms grew thinkers who wrestled with Euclid or Shakespeare; now, they often produce students dulled by screens and starved of the classics that sharpen the soul.

The Roots of Our Heritage

Our ancestors drew life from two streams of culture: folk tales and high art. Folk stories, born around the hearth in Celtic ballads or Germanic legends like those preserved by the Brothers Grimm, wove communities together through shared joys and sorrows. High culture took these roots and reached skyward: Homer's *Odyssey* (circa eighth century B.C.) wrestled with fate and human pride; Dante's *Divine Comedy* blended peasant speech with divine vision. These were not mere entertainments but mirrors of the eternal path, truth, beauty, and goodness that guide every true heart. From them sprang the Renaissance, or, closer to our time, J.R.R. Tolkien's *The Lord of the Rings*, which wove Anglo-Saxon grit and Arthurian light into a moral tapestry, proving depth can embrace the common touch. I recall my own youth, gathered with family over books and simple TV tales of our folk stories, not unlike the Shire's homely wisdom that sparked a love for Tolkien's enduring world.

The Rise of a Rootless Culture

Yet today, we turn from this heritage. Modern tales, shaped by corporate powers and artificial intelligence, often lack soul. Recent *Star Wars* films, like *The Rise of Skywalker*, chase nostalgia over myth, while *Rings of Power* flattens ancient lore to fit a market's mold. AI now conjures “art” think of young Skywalker’s face, digitally reborn in *The Mandalorian,* but it lacks the heart of human craft. This is no petty quibble over art; it reflects a deeper malaise. Behind-the-scenes, media moguls, tech giants, and hidden influencers wield algorithms to flood our minds with distractions, dulling our ability to question. Scandals like those tied to elite corruption, once whispered in shadows, flourish in this rootless age, where shallow stories mask graver moral failings.

Not all modern tales fail us. The original *Star Wars* trilogy, echoing Joseph Campbell’s heroic archetypes, stirred millions with its moral depth. Peter Jackson’s *The Lord of the Rings* brought Tolkien’s lore to life without betrayal, showing popular art can carry eternal truths. Even technology, used rightly say, to aid artisans, as Deloitte’s studies suggest, can serve the good. The fault lies not in screens or tools, but in their masters: powers that trade on fleeting pleasures, numbing us to deeper truths. Some argue modern media fosters creativity or community, but too often, it fragments our attention, leaving us prey to manipulation.

The Path to Renewal

The Path to Renewal The remedy lies in the old ways: classical education, rooted in the Christian West, which trains the soul to see clearly. Such schools, now serving 1.2M (ACCS 2025), surge toward 1.4M by 2035, a quiet rebellion against the factory model grinding obedient cogs. As Dr. Veith pens in A Handbook's foreword: "This path restores wisdom amid clamors." By forsaking classics, we've unleashed machine distractions, unraveling folk/high heritage.

This book traces this tale and offers hope. Chapter 1 explores how classical learning unites folk tales and high art. Chapter 2 charts the shift from Scholastic Realism (the belief in universal truths) to Nominalism (a focus on subjective ideas). Chapter 3 examines materialism's rise; Chapter 4, its dangerous dance with culture; Chapter 5, the hidden powers shaping our world; Chapter 6, the specter of a hollowed society; and Chapter 7, the path to renewal through Homer, Beowulf, Arthur's knights, and Tolkien's rings. Together, we seek not just loss, but the hope of a joyous turn into a restored garden, blooming with truth and beauty.

Chapter 1: The Power of Classical Education: Uniting Folk and High Culture

Classical education, at its core, represents a time-honored approach to learning that seeks to form the whole person, mind, body, and soul through a structured pursuit of truth, goodness, and beauty. Rooted in the ancient traditions of Greece and Rome, and later enriched by Western Christian thought, it revolves around the Trivium: grammar (mastering the building blocks of language and knowledge), logic (developing the ability to reason critically and discern truth), and rhetoric (cultivating eloquent expression to persuade and inspire). This framework, combined with the Socratic method of questioning and dialogue, and immersion in the Great Books, encouraged students to engage deeply with the world's intellectual heritage. Far from being an elitist relic, classical education fostered an appreciation for both folk culture, the communal, mythic stories that ground us in shared human experiences and high culture, the elevated works of philosophy, literature, and art that challenge us to transcend the ordinary.

The Trivium in Practice

The Trivium's practical application unfolds dynamically in a classical classroom, fostering thinkers who bridge folk and high culture. The Trivium's a three-step method from ancient times that teaches students to learn, think, and speak well, includes grammar (mastering facts), logic (reasoning clearly), and rhetoric (expressing ideas persuasively).

In the **grammar stage**, students build a cultural vocabulary by memorizing foundational knowledge, much like apprentices learning a trade. For example, at a Consortium for Classical and Lutheran Education (CCLE) school like Memorial Lutheran School in Houston, Texas, students chant Martin Luther's Small Catechism, including the Ten Commandments, in rhythmic call-and-response sessions to internalize Christian moral teachings (*CCLE Journal*, Vol. XVI, 2023). They also memorize Latin verb conjugations (e.g., *amo, amas, amat*) and recite passages from *The Aeneid* by Virgil, such as Aeneas's founding myth, grounding them in narratives that resist the fleeting allure of 2025's viral memes.

In the **logic stage**, students sharpen analytical skills, dissecting arguments and identifying fallacies. At an ACCS-affiliated school like Veritas Academy in Austin, Texas, students engage in Socratic seminars analyzing the moral complexity of Achilles's pride in Homer's *Iliad*, debating whether his actions align with Christian virtues of humility (ACCS, *2023 Annual Report*). They might also critique a 2025 social media campaign's *post hoc* fallacy, such as a tech ad claiming "buy this phone, and you'll succeed," comparing it to Achilles's flawed reasoning driven by hubris. This exercise, rooted in CCLE's logic curriculum, fosters critical media literacy, vital when 80% of social media content is projected to be AI-generated by 2025 (Deloitte, *Digital Media Trends 2024*).

The **rhetoric stage** empowers students to articulate insights persuasively. At Wittenberg Academy, a CCLE-accredited online school, a 10th-grader might deliver an oration defending C.S. Lewis's portrayal of courage in *The Lion, the Witch and the Wardrobe,* specifically Aslan's sacrifice against the simplified heroism in *Avengers: Infinity War*, where spectacle overshadows moral depth. In a structured debate, students argue whether Augustine's concept of *ordo amoris* (*On Christian Doctrine*, Book I, Ch. 27) supports prioritizing duty over desire in *Sir Gawain and the Green Knight*, using Gawain's acceptance of the Green Knight's challenge as evidence. This progression weaves folk tales' emotional resonance with high culture's philosophical depth, creating thinkers who navigate contemporary challenges.

In 2025, the Trivium counters digital distractions, as noted in the Pew Research Center's 2023 report showing that teenagers spend 7 hours daily on screens, undermining engagement with authentic narratives. A 2023 ACCS report, based on Classical Learning Test (CLT) scores, reveals classical students score 15–20% higher in critical thinking than public school peers, with Socratic seminars on *The Iliad* or Augustine's *Confessions* boosting engagement and moral reasoning. By blending folk traditions like scriptural chants with intellectual rigor from Great Books, the Trivium equips students to resist 2025's cultural downgrade, uniting earthy wisdom with the pursuit of truth. This approach directly challenges non-denominationalism's tendency to prioritize personal experience over communal doctrine, as seen in trend-driven megachurches that often sideline the creeds and sacraments central to historic Christianity. As Saint Paul urged, "hold fast to the traditions" (2 Thessalonians 2:15), and the Trivium ensures students are grounded in the apostolic faith, fostering unity and resilience against secularism's isolating lies.

Cicero and the Baptism of Roman Eloquence

Let us not shrink from naming one of the noblest of the pagans whom the Church has long plundered for her own: Marcus Tullius Cicero, the Roman orator whose voice still echoes through the corridors of Western rhetoric. In an age when the tongue has been tamed by algorithmic brevity and the public square reduced to the flicker of thumbs and outrage, Cicero stands as a towering reminder of what eloquence ordered toward virtue can accomplish. He was no Christian. Yet the Holy Spirit, who scatters seed even among the heathen, used this man's disciplined art to prepare the soil for the Gospel's reception.

Augustine himself confesses in the Confessions that it was Cicero's Hortensius which first kindled in his youthful soul a burning love for wisdom. It turned him from mere rhetoric toward the pursuit of truth. "That book," he writes, "changed my affections… I began to rise up to return to Thee." Here is the pattern: the Church does not fear the best of pagan learning. She takes it captive, circumcises it, and sets it to serve the proclamation of Christ crucified. Cicero's five canons of rhetoric (invention, arrangement, style, memory, delivery) became, in the hands of Augustine and later masters, the very scaffolding of Christian preaching and apologetics.

In the logic and rhetoric stages of the Trivium, where our children are trained to dissect fallacies and speak truth persuasively, Cicero belongs by right. His *De Oratore* sets forth the ideal orator as a man of comprehensive wisdom, moral integrity, and commanding eloquence—one who can move the soul not by manipulation but by ordering the affections toward the good. Read alongside Hooker's defense of reasoned persuasion in *Of the Laws of Ecclesiastical Polity*, or Lewis's own Ciceronian clarity in *Mere Christianity*, Cicero teaches our youth that words are not neutral tools but moral acts. To speak well is to imitate the Logos who spoke creation into being and who still speaks through His Church.

When our rhetoric-stage students stand before their peers to defend Aslan's costly grace against the cheap heroism of modern blockbusters, or to argue from natural law against the therapeutic tyranny that silences dissent in boardrooms and classrooms, they stand in a line that stretches back through Hooker, Augustine, and (yes) through Cicero himself. Let them read his *De Officiis* to grasp the duties of the just man in public life; let them study his *Catilinarian Orations* to feel the moral thunder of one who dared name corruption in the highest places. In so doing, they will learn that eloquence divorced from virtue is mere sophistry, but eloquence wedded to truth becomes a hammer that shatters idols and a trumpet that summons souls to repentance.

The nominalist age would have us believe that speech is but power, that persuasion is coercion dressed in silk. Cicero, though he knew not Christ, knew better: the true orator speaks because the soul, illumined by reason and virtue, cannot be silent when the commonwealth is imperiled. How much more, then, should the Christian orator, formed in the grammar of grace, sharpened by logic, and crowned with rhetoric, proclaim the greater commonwealth of the Kingdom? Let Cicero take his place beside Aquinas and Luther in our classrooms, not as master, but as servant. Plunder him gladly, baptize his gifts, and send forth a generation whose tongues are loosed to speak the unvarnished Word in an age that has forgotten how to listen.

Theological and Cultural Significance:

The Trivium's power lies not only in intellectual formation but in its alignment with Christendom's mission to form disciples who live for God's glory. By rooting students in Scripture and tradition, it counters the hyper-individualism of non-denominationalism, which often reduces faith to subjective experiences or celebrity-driven spectacles, as critiqued by thinkers like Cooper. For example, a student at Luther Classical College might study Luther's Freedom of a Christian alongside The Odyssey, learning how Christian liberty balances individual conscience with communal responsibility, resisting the secular mantra of "self as ultimate authority." This mirrors Bonhoeffer's call for "costly grace," where obedience to Christ unites believers in a shared mission, not isolated pursuits. By integrating folk hymns (e.g., "Amazing Grace") with high-culture works like Dante's Divine Comedy, classical education creates a cultural tapestry that reflects Romans 1:20's testimony to God's eternal attributes, equipping believers to rebuild a civilization rooted in divine truth.

Historical Foundations: Augustine's Vision

This integration of folk and high culture was not accidental but intentional, as seen in the works of key thinkers who shaped Western education. Saint Augustine, in his seminal On Christian Doctrine (De Doctrina Christiana, circa 397–426 AD), argued that classical learning, drawing from pagan liberal arts like grammar, rhetoric, and dialectic, should be harnessed for Christian purposes, such as interpreting Scripture and preaching effectively. Augustine viewed education as a tool to order one's affections rightly, defining virtue as ordo amoris, the "ordinate condition of the affections in which every object is accorded that kind and degree of love which is appropriate to it." He emphasized that without piety, learning leads to vanity, and without learning, piety results in an "unformed, undisciplined faith." For Augustine, classical education bridged folk elements, such as the everyday language and stories of the people, with the philosophical rigor of high culture, enabling believers to delight, instruct, and move others toward truth. This approach allowed students to appreciate the mythic tones of Homer's epics while applying them to Christian exegesis, fostering a holistic worldview that valued both communal heritage and eternal destiny. Augustine's influence extended beyond theory; in his Confessions, he recounts his own journey from youthful indulgence in folk entertainments like gladiatorial games to a profound embrace of high culture through Plato and Scripture, demonstrating how education can redeem and elevate personal experience.

Reformation and Education: Luther's Call

Building on this foundation, Martin Luther, in his 1524 treatise To the Councilmen of All Cities in Germany That They Establish and Maintain Christian Schools, called for widespread public education to counter cultural and moral decay. Luther argued that governments had a divine duty to educate all children, boys and girls alike, in the Gospel, classical languages (Latin, Greek, Hebrew), and liberal arts, so they could read Scripture independently and serve society wisely. He wrote, "And would to God that every town had a girls' school as well, where the girls would be taught the gospel for an hour every day either in German or in Latin," emphasizing that education was not merely utilitarian but essential for spiritual and civic formation. Luther warned that neglecting schools would lead to societal ruin, urging, "God has not given you your children and the means to support them simply so that you may do with them as you please, or raise them like epicures. You have been given children so that you may train them for God and for the good of society." By integrating folk culture's vernacular tales with high culture's classical texts, Luther's vision reformed education to produce principled citizens capable of resisting tyranny and corruption, much like the Reformation's challenge to ecclesiastical abuses. Luther's reforms had a lasting impact; they inspired the establishment of schools across Europe that blended local folk hymns and stories with rigorous study of ancient texts, creating communities resilient against the intellectual stagnation of the time.

Medieval Synthesis: Aquinas and Scholasticism

In the medieval period, this classical ethos was further embodied by figures like Thomas Aquinas, who in his *Summa Theologica* synthesized Aristotelian logic with Christian theology, drawing on folk parables from Scripture while engaging high-culture debates on ethics and metaphysics. For instance, in the *Summa Theologica* (I, q. 1, a. 5, ad 2), Aquinas explains that sacred doctrine "can in a sense depend upon the philosophical sciences, not as though it stood in need of them, but only in order to make its teaching clearer, for it accepts its principles not from other sciences, but immediately from God, by revelation. Therefore, it does not depend upon other sciences as upon the higher, but makes use of them as of the lesser, and as handmaidens." This illustrates how philosophy serves as a "handmaiden" to theology, clarifying revealed truths without supplanting them, thereby harmonizing reason and faith in a way that bridges high intellectual pursuits with the foundational wisdom of Scripture.

Aquinas's method of scholastic disputation, posing questions, objections, and resolutions, mirrored the Socratic dialogue, showing how classical education could harmonize the earthy wisdom of proverbs and legends with the lofty pursuits of philosophy. In *Summa Theologica* (I, q. 1, a. 8), he elaborates on this argumentative approach: "As other sciences do not argue in proof of their principles, but argue from their principles to demonstrate other truths in these sciences: so this doctrine does not argue in proof of its principles, which are the articles of faith, but from them it goes on to prove something else." Here, Aquinas employs logical disputation to build upon articles of faith, much like how folk parables in Scripture (e.g., the parables of Jesus) provide relatable, communal insights that are then elevated through philosophical analysis to address metaphysical questions, such as the nature of virtue or the existence of God.

This tradition ensured that education remained a bridge between the common people's lived experiences reflected in scriptural narratives and folk wisdom and the elite's scholarly endeavors, preventing the cultural silos that plague modern society. By integrating Aristotelian principles with Christian revelation, Aquinas's work exemplifies how classical education fosters a holistic formation, where students learn to apply reasoned argumentation to divine truths, drawing from both the accessible stories of the people and the rigorous debates of philosophers.

Modern Critiques: C.S. Lewis and Moral Formation

In the 20th century, C.S. Lewis echoed these sentiments in The Abolition of Man (1943), critiquing modern education's abandonment of objective values, what he called the "Tao," or natural law, in favor of subjective relativism. Lewis argued that true education must "irrigate deserts" rather than "cut down jungles," inculcating just sentiments to defend against false ones. He warned, "It is the doctrine of objective value, the belief that certain attitudes are really true, and others really false, to the kind of thing the universe is and which we are." Without this, education produces "men without chests," intellectually capable but morally hollow, vulnerable to manipulation. Lewis drew on classical and Christian traditions to advocate for an education that unites folk culture's instinctive virtues with high culture's rational pursuit of truth, ensuring students recognize universal morals amid cultural noise. Lewis's own works, such as The Chronicles of Narnia, exemplify this: they cloak profound Christian allegory in folk-like fairy tales, accessible to children yet rich with high-culture references to medieval romance and Platonic ideals, proving education's power to inspire across generations.

Contemporary Revival: Classical Lutheran Education

This rich tradition aligns with contemporary calls for renewal, as seen in *A Handbook for Classical Lutheran Education* by Chole Swope and the Consortium for Classical and Lutheran Education (CCLE). In the foreword by Dr. Gene Edward Veith, the book is described as explaining "what classical Lutheran education is and why it is needed today. It shows the connection between classical education and the Lutheran tradition." Swope's work integrates Lutheran theology, emphasizing scripture, grace, and vocation, with classical methods, arguing that such an education equips students to discern truth and uphold justice in a fallen world. It fosters moral and intellectual virtue, countering the materialism that dilutes cultural depth.

Building on this foundation, contemporary Lutheran theologians like Rev. Dr. Jordan B. Cooper further advocate for classical education as a solution to modern crises. As President of the American Lutheran Theological Seminary (ALTS) and host of the Just and Sinner podcast, Cooper emphasizes the Reformation roots of classical Lutheran education in works such as his 2022 presentation, "Solving Our Education Crisis." He critiques modern schooling for its focus on industrial productivity and hidden ideological agendas, such as promoting gender theories while neglecting humanities and character formation. Instead, Cooper draws on Martin Luther and Philip Melanchthon to promote a model that begins with home-based catechesis, extends to public Christian schools, and incorporates the Trivium (grammar, logic, rhetoric) and Quadrivium (arithmetic, geometry, music, astronomy). He argues that this approach raises "virtuous, educated individuals who know themselves, their world, and God," enabling independent inquiry into meaning and purpose. Cooper recommends Lutherans prioritize building schools as a ministry, blending monastic educational ideals with Protestant emphases on justification by faith, to counter 2025's digital and cultural distractions.

Modern initiatives like the Association of Classical Christian Schools (ACCS) build on this, with thousands of schools worldwide reviving the Trivium and Great Books curriculum, reporting higher student engagement and critical thinking skills compared to standardized models. Additionally, institutions like Luther Classical College offer associate's degrees in Lutheran theology and classical liberal arts, aiming to form students in conservative Lutheran traditions. These efforts demonstrate that classical education isn't outdated but urgently relevant, helping students navigate digital distractions by rooting them in enduring narratives.

Contemporary and Historical Revival: Classical Anglican Education

Following the Lutheran revival, Classical Anglican Education offers another vibrant expression of the classical model, deeply rooted in the English Reformation and Anglicanism's *via media*, which balances Scripture, tradition, and reason.

Richard Hooker (1554–1600), often called the father of Anglicanism, laid a theological foundation for classical education in his *Of the Laws of Ecclesiastical Polity* (Book V, 1597). Writing during the English Reformation, Hooker defended the Church of England's structure using classical rhetoric and Aristotelian logic, blending folk elements like the vernacular *Book of Common Prayer* with high-culture scholarship. He argued that education should cultivate wisdom for governance and piety, stating, "The end of all learning is to know God, and out of that knowledge to love and imitate Him." For Hooker, studying classical texts such as Plato and Cicero alongside Scripture was essential to forming rational, virtuous citizens capable of resisting tyranny. His approach mirrored the Trivium: grammar through mastering biblical and classical languages, logic via structured disputations, and rhetoric in crafting persuasive sermons. Anglican schools, such as Eton and Winchester, adopted this model, teaching Latin and Greek to connect students with their cultural heritage, from English folk ballads to Virgil's *Aeneid.* Hooker's vision ensured education bridged the earthy faith of common people with the philosophical depth of scholars, fostering a holistic worldview.

Today, Anglican classical schools, such as St. Dunstan's Academy and Good Shepherd School, integrate Hooker's emphasis on ordered learning with a literary approach. They combine daily *Book of Common Prayer* liturgies rooted in folk worship with rigorous study. The Anglican Schools Association (ASA), operating under the RE National Education Board of the Anglican Church in North America, reports a 10% enrollment increase across its member schools from 2020 to 2024, reflecting growing demand for classical Anglican education. Programs like Scholé Academy's Canterbury House of Studies, which serves over 500 homeschooling families in 2025, offer Trivium-based curricula infused with Anglican theology, emphasizing spiritual formation through daily worship and classical texts. These schools, part of the Anglican Province of America, Reformed Episcopal Church, and Anglican Church in North America, also provide accreditation and teacher certification to ensure academic and spiritual excellence. ASA's partnership with a national Christian educational foundation supports new school launches, with five new parochial schools established in 2024, focusing on affordable resources for leadership and fundraising. These initiatives counter the Prussian model's standardization, fostering thinkers who can navigate 2025's cultural downgrade by uniting folk hymns and stories with high-culture rhetoric.

Classical Anglican Education, from Hooker's Reformation-era synthesis to Lewis's modern literary apologetics, bridges folk and high culture to form discerning, virtuous individuals. By grounding students in communal traditions and elevating them through intellectual rigor, it offers a powerful antidote to materialism, aligning with the broader revival of classical education to restore cultural depth.

2025 Anglican Surge: St. Anselm's Academy Rises Amid Ashes

As the old Prussian model echoes standardize souls, Anglican revival blazes. St. Anselm's Academy (Dallas, est. Sept 2025) launches with 250 students, oversubscribed 2x, blending Book of Common Prayer folk liturgies with Trivium rigor. Rhetoric seniors orate Hooker vs. 2025 TikTok "prayer challenges": "Vernacular prayer grounds; algorithmic 'manifestation' elevates self over God." ASA's Oct 2025 update: +12% enrollment (from 10%), 7 new schools (up from 5). Scholé Canterbury now 650 families (+30%)

The Synergy of Folk and High Culture

The synergy of folk and high culture in classical education is evident in how it complements communal grounding with intellectual elevation. Folk tales, like the Anglo-Saxon myths in Beowulf or the chivalric quests in Chrétien de Troyes's Arthurian romances, provide raw, relatable narratives of heroism and community, while high culture Shakespeare's tragedies or Chrétien's own courtly verse refines these into profound explorations of sin, redemption, and human nature. Tolkien's The Lord of the Rings exemplifies this blend, drawing on folk traditions and high literary craft to create a mythic world that grapples with philosophical themes like stewardship and sacrifice, appealing to both heart and mind. Similarly, Virgil's Aeneid merges Roman folk legends of founding myths with Homeric high epic structure, exploring duty, piety, and empire in ways that influenced Christian thinkers. These examples, especially Chrétien's transformation of crude Grail legends into the first psychological novel, show how classical education trains students to see the interconnectedness of cultural layers, fostering empathy and wisdom.

This synergy extends to Anglican traditions, where Charles Wesley's hymns, like "Hark! The Herald Angels Sing" (1739), elevate folk melodies into theological poetry, blending the communal joy of carols with high-culture reflections on Christ's divinity. Similarly, John Donne's metaphysical poetry, such as Holy Sonnets (c. 1609–1611), weds vernacular passion with classical allusions to Cicero and Jerome, inviting readers to wrestle with sin and grace. These works, rooted in Anglicanism's via media, show how folk roots can be refined into timeless art, a process classical education mirrors by guiding students from storytelling to philosophical inquiry.

The Prussian Model: A Contrast

In stark contrast, the Prussian model developed in the late 18th century under Frederick the Great and adopted widely in the 19th prioritizes standardization, efficiency, and obedience to produce workers for industrial societies. Influenced by Johann Fichte's ideas of state-controlled education to mold loyal citizens, it groups students by age rather than ability, emphasizes rote learning over critical inquiry, and sidelines humanities for practical skills, disconnecting learners from their cultural roots. This model, as critiqued by thinkers like Luther and Lewis, fosters conformity rather than conviction, making society ripe for the shallow pop culture we see today, where depth is sacrificed for accessibility and profit. Its legacy persists in modern public schooling, where standardized tests prioritize measurable outcomes over moral formation, leading to generations alienated from their heritage.

The Prussian model originated amid profound national crisis, particularly after Prussia's humiliating defeat by Napoleon in 1806, which exposed weaknesses in military, society, and education. Johann Gottlieb Fichte, a philosopher and key architect, delivered his "Addresses to the German Nation" in 1808, advocating for a compulsory, state-run education system to rebuild national strength through uniformity and patriotism. Fichte envisioned education not as a pursuit of individual enlightenment but as a tool for socialization, instilling absolute obedience to the state and suppressing Enlightenment ideals of liberty that he blamed for Prussia's downfall. By centralizing control, the system aimed to create obedient soldiers, factory workers, and civil servants who prioritized collective duty over personal conviction.

Critics highlight the model's shady intentions: it was explicitly designed for indoctrination and social control, breaking familial influences to mold children into compliant nationals. Fichte proposed removing children from parental oversight to ensure loyalty to the state, viewing education as statecraft rather than soul craft. This approach suppressed critical thinking and cultural roots, favoring rote memorization and hierarchy to serve industrial and military needs, echoing how Prussian teachers acted as "military occupiers" to impose nationalism and erase local identities. In 2025, this legacy amplifies cultural downgrade, as standardized systems leave students vulnerable to algorithmic pop culture, lacking the discernment fostered by classical methods.

Cultural Impact: Tolkien and Modern Media

A poignant example is the adaptation of Tolkien's works. LOTR's folk/high triumph in the books and Peter Jackson's films (2001–

2003) preserved intricate lore and moral complexity, achieving massive success without compromise. Yet, The Rings of Power (2022) simplifies Tolkien's Second Age into a visually stunning but narratively flattened spectacle, criticized for lacking the original's soul and philosophical weight. Users often decry its "woke" insertions and rushed plotting that ignore Tolkien's emphasis on linguistic depth and mythic authenticity. This downgrade mirrors how the Prussian model's legacy leaves audiences less equipped to demand or appreciate the cultural synergy that classical education once nurtured. Other franchises suffer similarly; for instance, the Marvel Cinematic Universe, while entertaining, often reduces complex comic book folklore to formulaic blockbusters, prioritizing merchandising over the moral introspection found in original stories like those of Captain America grappling with authority and freedom.

Conclusion: A Call for Renewal

We stand in the year of our Lord 2026, amid the smoking ruins of a culture that once confessed with its cathedrals and its constitutions that man is made for God. Relativism has entered the sanctuary, removed the ancient landmarks, and set up its own altar. And the people, our children, wander in this wilderness, feeding on the husks of algorithmic husks, knowing neither who they are nor Whose they are.

There is but one remedy: the deliberate, disciplined, joyous recovery of classical Christian education, the education of Augustine and Alfred, of Hooker and Hobart, of Luther and Lewis. This is no mere pedagogical preference; it is the ordained means by which the Church Militant here on earth re-claims its stolen heritage and re-arms the children.

For what is classical education but the grammar of grace? It teaches a child to chant the Creed before he can curse the culture. It teaches him to stand in the presence of Achilles' wrath and Aslan's sacrifice and, by the light of both, to recognize the wrath of the Lamb who was slain. It teaches him that truth is not a mood, virtue is not a vibe, and beauty is not a filter.

While the Prussian parade-ground still marches souls in lock-step toward the relativist that is fleeting, the platoons of classical schools are quietly raising up a generation that can say, with Richard Hooker, "Order is heaven's first law," and mean it with their lives. They are learning to detect the false infinities of the metaverse by first measuring the true infinity of the Triune God.

Every Socratic question asked in a seventh-grade classroom is a nail in the coffin of "my truth." Every senior thesis that dares to defend the permanent things is a banner planted on the ruins of the transitory.

The need is urgent; the time is now. For the Church that forgets how to educate the young is the Church that has already conceded the future to the heathen. But the Church that recovers the Trivium and the Quadrivium, the Great Books and the Greater Book, the catechism and the creed, the hymn and the heroic lay that Church shall see her children rise up and call her blessed, and her enemies shall be found liars unto her.

Chapter 2: From Scholastic Realism to Nominalism: The Philosophical Roots of Cultural Fragmentation

Picture a mighty oak, its roots deep in the soil of Western Christian thought, its branches laden with the fruits of truth, goodness, and beauty, sheltering a civilization that drew life from its shade. This was the world of Scholastic realism, where thinkers like Bonaventure: The Seraphic Doctor and Aquinas anchored reason and faith in a divine order, forging a worldview that harmonized the communal wisdom of Christian tradition with the intellectual rigor of classical philosophy. Through classical education's steady hand, this vision trained souls to love rightly, aligning human affections with God's eternal truths. Yet, like subtle winds that erode even the stoutest trunk, a shift began in the medieval twilight, a turn toward nominalism, where universals like virtue and beauty were stripped of their eternal weight, reduced to mere names shaped by human whim. This philosophical pivot, subtle yet seismic, uprooted the foundations of the Christian mind, scattering its branches into the storms of materialism and relativism that now buffet our age. In this chapter, we trace how the move from Scholastic realism to nominalism set the stage for the cultural downgrade we face in 2025, a world where corporate algorithms and shallow pop culture, from the trauma-stripped spectacle of Final Fantasy VII Remake to fleeting TikTok trends, thrive in a society unmoored from objective truth. By understanding this fracture, rooted in the rejection of God's transcendent order, we uncover the philosophical roots of our crisis and glimpse the path to renewal through a return to the eternal verities that once held us fast.

Scholastic Realism: The Foundation of Classical Christian Thought

In the grand edifice of Western Christianity, Scholastic realism stood as the cornerstone, a philosophical and theological framework that affirmed the reality of universals—those eternal essences such as goodness, justice, and beauty—as objective reflections of God's mind, embedded in the very fabric of creation. This was no abstract speculation but a living vision that permeated education, culture, and daily life, ensuring that the pursuit of knowledge led inexorably toward the divine. At its heart lay the conviction that the world is intelligible because it participates in the transcendent forms of truth, allowing reason and faith to walk hand in hand, much as the Apostle Paul urged in 2 Timothy 2:15: "Do your best to present yourself to God as one approved, a worker who has no need to be ashamed, rightly handling the word of truth."

Even today, when a man stands speechless before a crimson sunset spilling over a mountain waterfall, or when a new mother's heart is suddenly reordered around a helpless infant, something older than culture stirs. Why do these sights and experiences strike nearly every human soul as **beautiful** and **morally reorienting**, regardless of tribe or era? Scholastic realism has the answer: they are **theophanies**—visible splinters of God's infinite claritas and bonitas breaking in on us. Aquinas taught that beauty is *id quod visum placet*—that which, being seen, pleases—because it bears the objective marks of proportion, integrity, and radiance (Summa Theologiae I, q. 5, a. 4). A waterfall roars with claritas; a mother's self-sacrificial love images God's own agape. Romans

1:20 and 2:14–15 are not poetry but ontology: "God's invisible qualities… have been clearly seen" in creation, and "the requirements of the law are written on [all] hearts." These universal reactions are not cultural conditioning; they are **created participation in divine universals**. Nominalism will later call them mere "names." Realism knows them as fingerprints of the living God.

Saint Augustine, whose Confessions and On Christian Doctrine bridged antiquity and the medieval world, exemplified this realism in its early flowering. For Augustine, knowledge was an ascent of the soul toward God, where universals like wisdom and virtue were not human inventions but illuminations from the eternal Light. In his De Magistro (The Teacher, 389 AD), he argued that true understanding comes not from words alone but from the inner Teacher, Christ, who reveals the realities behind signs. This realist ontology underpinned his educational ideal: the liberal arts, grammar, logic, rhetoric, and beyond, served to purify the soul so that love of the Creator outshone all lesser goods. Augustine's realism harmonized the communal wisdom of Scripture and patristic tradition with the rigor of Platonic philosophy, enabling believers to "plunder the Egyptians" (Exodus 3:22), drawing pagan truths like geometry and music into the service of Christian exegesis. In the classroom, this meant students encountering the mythic echoes of Homer not as pagan idols but as pointers to divine providence, training them to discern universal truths amid cultural diversity.

Thomas Aquinas brought this realism to its scholastic zenith in the 13th century, synthesizing Aristotelian empiricism with Augustinian theology in works like the Summa Theologica (1265–1274). For Aquinas, universals exist both ante rem (in God's mind as archetypes) and in re (in created things as essences), making the world a sacrament of divine reason. "Beauty is that which pleases when seen," he wrote, rooted in clarity, proportion, and integrity, objective qualities mirroring the Creator's harmony. This framework elevated education as a participation in God's intellectus, where the Trivium and Quadrivium peeled back the veils of particularity to reveal universal principles. Aquinas's method of disputation, posing questions, objections, and resolutions, mirrored Socratic dialogue while grounding it in revelation, allowing students to engage folk parables from the Gospels (like the Prodigal Son's communal themes) alongside high metaphysics, fostering a holistic worldview that resisted fragmentation. As Gene Edward Veith notes in his foreword to A Handbook for Classical Lutheran Education, this synthesis "shows the connection between classical education and the Christian tradition," ensuring that learning formed not just the mind but the moral chest.

This realist foundation permeated medieval culture, from the stained-glass cathedrals of Chartres, where geometric proportions embodied divine universals, to the vernacular hymns of Hildegard of Bingen, blending folk melody with theological depth. In education, it birthed universities like Paris and Oxford, where scholars debated universals not as ivory-tower disputes but as vital to ethics, law, and governance. Realism affirmed that human laws and virtues derived from natural law, God's eternal reason imprinted on creation (Romans 2:14-15), providing a bulwark against arbitrary power. Thus, Scholastic realism was the soil from which classical Christian education flourished, uniting folk heritage's earthy wisdom with high culture's aspirational pursuit, equipping generations to navigate a fallen world with discernment and devotion.

Aristotle and the Baptized Logic of the Real

Among the treasures the Church has most boldly plundered from the Egyptians stands Aristotle, the Philosopher whose logic and metaphysics the medieval doctors, above all Thomas Aquinas, took captive and set to serve divine truth. In an age when nominalism has reduced universals to mere names and the modern mind treats reality as plastic to human will, Aristotle reminds us that the world is intelligible because it is ordered by form, essence, and final cause. His hylomorphism, matter informed by form, grounds the very realism the Church has defended against Ockham's razor: things have real natures, not arbitrary labels; goodness, truth, and beauty are not subjective projections but objective participations in the divine mind.

Aquinas, in the *Summa Theologica*, weds Aristotle's categories to revelation without compromise: the Philosopher's four causes become handmaids to theology, his ethics of virtue a prelude to the theological virtues, his natural law a reflection of eternal law. "Grace does not destroy nature," Aquinas declares, "but perfects it." Thus Aristotle's teleology, the notion that every thing has an end toward which it is directed, finds its fulfillment in the beatific vision, where the soul rests in the contemplation of God Himself.

In the logic stage of the Trivium, where students learn to reason clearly and detect fallacies, Aristotle's Organon belongs by right. His categories, syllogisms, and distinction between substance and accident train the mind to grasp what is real amid the flux of appearances. Read alongside Augustine's insistence that truth is eternal and unchanging, or Hooker's appeal to reason illumined by Scripture, Aristotle teaches our youth that the world is not chaos but cosmos, ordered, knowable, good. When they dissect the post hoc fallacies of modern advertising or debate the hubris of Achilles against the humility of Christ, they stand in a line that runs through Aquinas back to the Stagirite himself.

Let the nominalist age mock "dead white males"; we know better. Aristotle, though he knew not the Incarnation, glimpsed the rational order that the Logos imprinted on creation. Plunder him gladly, baptize his gifts, and send forth a generation equipped to name things truly, to love them rightly, and to order society toward the common good. In so doing, we do not bow to pagan wisdom; we make it bow to the greater Wisdom who is Christ, in whom all things hold together.

Scholastic Realism and the Birth of Modern Science: Rational Order as Divine Mandate

Forget the old myth of a "Dark Ages" Church crushing curiosity. Scholastic realism gave modern science the **ground it needed to grow**. The same belief that universals—things like *cause*, *motion*, and *intelligibility*—are real in God's mind and woven into creation meant we *had* to study them. If the universe is a clear sign of God's reason, exploring it is an act of worship, no less than taking communion. As Alfred North Whitehead put it in *Science and the Modern World* (1925), medieval faith in a lawful cosmos "exemplifying general principles" was the one thing no other worldview gave science.

That conviction created the **university itself**. Bologna (c. 1088), Paris (c. 1150), Oxford (c. 1167), and Cambridge (c. 1209) started under papal charters. They trained priests in theology but *required* natural philosophy first. Students read Aristotle's *Physics*, *On the Heavens*, and *Metaphysics*—translated in Church schools at Toledo and Salerno—because ideas like *substance* and *form* were tools to read creation's language. The Church needed exact dates for Easter, so it paid for star-watching and better math. Pope Sylvester II (Gerbert of Aurillac, r. 999–1003) brought Arabic numerals and the astrolabe to Europe.

The Scholastic **debate method** was early science in action. A question (*Does the sky move?*), objections (*It seems so*), authorities (*But Scripture says…*), a reasoned answer, then rebuttals. Sound familiar? It's the shape of a modern lab report. Roger Bacon, OP (c. 1214–1292), in *Opus Majus* (1267), called for "crucial experiments" to test ideas and said math is the "door and key" to nature because numbers share God's eternity. His Franciscan friend Bonaventure (1221–1274) saw every experiment as a path back to the First Cause.

These were textbook lessons, not side projects. The Merton "Calculators" turned change into math because realism said *quantity* is real, not just a label. Oresme drew speed-time rectangles in 1350; Galileo read the same tradition in Padua. Pierre Duhem's massive *Le Système du Monde* (1913–1959) shows hundreds of such pages. The 1277 Condemnation—banning claims that God *must* follow Aristotle—actually *freed* thinkers to test "what if" models.

Even God's freedom helped: if He can override nature, we need experiments to see what He *did* choose. Robert Grosseteste (c. 1175–1253), bishop and Oxford founder, said light spreads by math because geometry mirrors God's clarity. His student Bacon built the first pinhole camera. Albertus Magnus (c. 1200–1280), Dominican bishop, hiked mountains to catalog rocks by their real *essence*—fieldwork rooted in realism.

Nominalism cut the cord. Ockham's razor, meant to guard God's freedom, said universals live only in our heads. Cause became habit, not connection. Buridan's impetus turned from real force to mental shortcut. By 1500, textbooks at Erfurt and Wittenberg taught doubt about nature's certainty—setting up Hume's "just patterns" and a clockwork world with no purpose. The same schools that launched science now launched Locke's blank-slate mind and Bacon's "idols" of mere sensation. The knowable order—because it shared God's mind—shrank to guesswork.

Bottom line: Scholastic realism didn't just *allow* science—it demanded it. Nominalism, by snapping the link between things and their meaning, snapped the reason the Scientific Revolution happened in Christian Europe and nowhere else. The oak's deepest root was simple: to know the world is to love its Maker. Cut that, and the branches rot into the relativist weeds we see and live through today.

The Rise of Nominalism

The harmony of Scholastic realism began to fray in the late medieval period with the rise of nominalism, a philosophical shift spearheaded by key figures like William of Ockham (c. 1287–1347). Ockham, a Franciscan friar exiled from Avignon for his critiques of papal authority, wielded his famous "razor," a principle of parsimony that shaves away unnecessary entities to argue against the bloated metaphysics of realism. For Ockham, universals like goodness and beauty were not objective reflections of divine order but *nomina* names or labels invented by human minds to group particulars, with no independent existence beyond linguistic convenience. This was no mere academic quibble; it stemmed from a profound theological voluntarism, emphasizing God's absolute, arbitrary will over a rational, knowable creation. By denying universals as real, Ockham sought to safeguard divine omnipotence: if universals existed eternally in God's mind (as realists claimed), they might constrain His freedom to create or will as He pleased. Instead, God could ordain truths *ex nihilo*, making morality and even logic contingent on His fiat rather than inherent essences. Unlike realism, which held that universals like goodness and beauty exist objectively as part of God's eternal order, nominalism argued that universals are merely *nomina* names or labels created by human minds to categorize particulars, with no independent existence. Ockham asserted in his *Summa Logicae* (c. 1323) that only individual things exist, and abstract concepts like justice or virtue are mental constructs, useful but not rooted in divine reality. This view, while aiming to protect God's sovereignty through voluntarism emphasizing His arbitrary will over intellect, led to fideism (faith detached from reason) and skepticism, as it severed the intelligible link between creation and Creator. The immediate fallout was seismic: nominalism fueled the *via moderna* in universities like Oxford and Paris, eroding the scholastic synthesis and contributing to the Western Schism (1378–1417), where rival popes vied for power amid debates over divine will versus natural law. It also sowed seeds of doubt in ecclesiastical authority, as Ockham's excommunication highlighted how nominalist skepticism could challenge not just metaphysics but the very structures of Christendom.

The consequences rippled through history, reshaping Western thought and culture in ways that resonate into 2025. Nominalism's fractures influenced the Reformation: Martin Luther, in his 1524 treatise *To the Councilmen of All Cities in Germany That They Establish and Maintain Christian Schools*, critiqued nominalism's excesses for undermining scholastic synthesis, yet drew from realist commitments to Scripture as objective truth to advocate for education grounded in classical languages and the Gospel. Luther's own nominalist training at Erfurt (under figures like Gabriel Biel) left him wrestling with its fideistic pull, but he ultimately rejected its extremes, insisting on a scriptural realism in which God's Word anchors universals such as grace and justification. This ambivalence paved the way for empiricism in figures like Francis Bacon and John Locke. Bacon's *Novum*

Organum (1620) championed inductive observation of particulars, while Locke's *Essay Concerning Human Understanding* (1689) reduced ideas to individual sensory impressions, feeding the materialism that would dominate Enlightenment thought. By prioritizing the empirical over the metaphysical, nominalism uprooted the transcendent anchors of Western culture, setting the stage for relativism and the utilitarian education models that followed. As historian Michael Allen Gillespie argues in *The Theological Origins of Modernity* (2008, still influential in 2025 debates), nominalism's "turn this world on its head" by making human will the measure of reality, echoing in today's postmodern flux where truth is "constructed" rather than discovered.

Long-Term Cultural and Theological Impact:

Nominalism's legacy profoundly shaped the trajectory of Western Christendom, undermining the objective foundations of truth, goodness, and beauty that your book seeks to reclaim. By reducing universals to mere names, nominalism eroded the belief that creation reflects God's eternal order. This shift paved the way for a fragmented worldview where individual perceptions trump shared reality, fueling the hyper-individualism critiqued in your conclusion. In 2025, this manifests in the subjective faith of non-denominationalism, where personal experience often overshadows the apostolic tradition Saint Paul urged believers to "hold fast" (2 Thessalonians 2:15). For example, trend-driven megachurches, prioritizing charismatic sermons over creeds like the Nicene Creed, reflect nominalism's skepticism of universal truths, lacking the moral conviction to resist secular relativism. Jordan B. Cooper, in *In Defense of the True, the Good, and the Beautiful*, warns that this loss of transcendence leaves Christians vulnerable to cultural dogmas like consumerism or moral relativism.

Nominalism also birthed a cultural skepticism that challenges Christendom's unity. Dietrich Bonhoeffer, in The Cost of Discipleship, critiqued fideism's detachment of faith from reason, arguing that true discipleship demands obedience to Christ's objective truth, not subjective constructs. His resistance to Nazi ideology, a secular outworking of nominalist voluntarism, where human will dictated morality, parallels your call to resist 2025's "constructed" truths, such as social media campaigns claiming "beauty is in the eye of the beholder." This nominalist legacy undermines the objective beauty championed by Bonaventure and Aquinas, who saw it as a reflection of God's order. N.T. Wright's critique of secularism's "split-level epistemology" (The New Testament and the People of God, 1992) aligns with your argument: nominalism's denial of universals fragments knowledge, leaving faith unmoored from reason and vulnerable to secular ideologies like those in public schools, which prioritize utility over virtue (per your Prussian model critique).

Contemporary Manifestations and Resistance:

In 2025, nominalism's influence permeates education and culture, amplifying the need for classical Christian education to restore Christendom's foundations. The utilitarian Prussian model, rooted in nominalist empiricism, produces students who excel in standardized tests but lack the moral framework to question AI-driven narratives or corporate media's simplified stories (e.g., Disney's live-action Snow White (2025) gutting the Grimm tale's archetypal depth, innocence, sacrifice, redemptive love for focus-grouped slogans). At Veritas Academy, students in a rhetoric-stage seminar might debate how nominalism's legacy in Locke's empiricism fuels 2025's "post-truth" culture, where social media algorithms shape perceptions of morality (e.g., a viral ad equating happiness with consumption). By studying Aquinas's Summa

Theologica alongside Scripture, they learn to defend objective truth against relativism, embodying Paul's call to "test everything" (1 Thessalonians 5:21). Similarly, at Luther Classical College, students explore Luther's rejection of nominalist fideism in The Freedom of a Christian, applying it to critique non-denominational churches that sideline sacraments for emotional worship, reinforcing your argument that such trends are unsustainable without apostolic anchors.

The church can resist nominalism's legacy by reviving classical education's synthesis of faith and reason, as your book advocates. For example, a CCLE school might host a festival where students perform Wesley's "Hark! The Herald Angels Sing" alongside reciting Lancelot Andrewes's Preces Privatae, blending folk worship with high-culture theology to counter nominalism's fragmentation. Andrewes's private devotions, intimate, scripturally saturated prayers such as "Blessed art Thou, O Lord… who hast brought us to the beginning of this day," model how personal piety can be both profoundly deep and theologically rich, inspiring even solitary moments to echo the grandeur of public liturgy. By fostering thinkers who see God's truth in both creation and Scripture, classical education restores the realist vision that nominalism shattered.

Cultural and Educational Ramifications

Nominalism's subtle revolution fragmented culture profoundly: folk traditions, once grounded in universal virtues, lost their objective mooring, becoming subjective stories open to reinterpretation. High culture, from Sophocles' Antigone, where the clash between divine law and human edict assumes an objective moral order, to Shakespeare's tragedies, devolved into mere aesthetic preferences, stripped of eternal truths. In 2025,

Disney's The Acolyte (2024), a Star Wars series, exemplifies this nominalist erosion. By reimagining the Force's universal moral archetypes rooted in George Lucas's Campbell-inspired myth of good versus evil as relativistic character arcs driven by personal vendettas, the series fragments the saga's mythic unity. Fans in 2024 criticized its focus on individual identities over objective moral frameworks, lamenting a departure from the Jedi's transcendent ideals. This shift, reducing the Force to subjective "labels" tailored to viewer preferences, mirrors nominalism's denial of universal essences, enabling 2025's cultural downgrade where algorithms prioritize profit-driven spectacle over the shared truths realism once upheld.

Educationally, nominalism eroded the Trivium's unity, redirecting learning toward utility and experience. The Prussian model, influenced by Johann Fichte's nominalist-inspired statecraft in his *Addresses to the German Nation* (1808), emphasized standardization and obedience over critical discernment, producing intellectually capable but morally hollow, vulnerable to manipulation. In 2025 classrooms, this manifests as AI tutors prioritizing "personalized learning" (e.g., adaptive apps generating individualized math "truths" without universal principles), fostering relativism over rigorous logic. ACCS data indicates classical students outperform public peers by 15–20% in critical thinking metrics (e.g., SAT/CLT reasoning), as nominalist curricula leave youth adrift in a sea of algorithmic "facts," unable to discern objective beauty amid TikTok's fleeting trends. Francis Schaeffer, in *How Should We Then Live?* (1976), echoed this, warning that nominalism's humanism leads to cultural despair, where art and education serve self rather than divine order. Recent analyses, like those in *Thesis Eleven* (2025), link this to AI's "magical nominalism," where generated content floods media, eroding shared cultural anchors and amplifying isolation in a post-universal age.

Biblical and Theological Critique

This philosophical shift can be framed as spiritual decay, echoing Romans 1:21–25: "For although they knew God, they did not honor him as God or give thanks to him, but they became futile in their thinking, and their foolish hearts were darkened. Claiming to be wise, they became fools, and exchanged the glory of the immortal God for images resembling mortal man..." Nominalism exchanges God's objective glory revealed in creation's universal order (Psalm 19:1: "The heavens declare the glory of God") for human constructs, undermining the imago Dei by making us doubt universal truths like divine beauty and goodness. It acts as Satan's tool to fragment our perception of God, reducing His attributes to subjective whims rather than eternal realities. In 2025, this echoes in AI's "god-like" generation of realities e.g., deepfake Scriptures or personalized theologies mirroring nominalism's voluntarism by letting algorithms "will" truths unbound by divine essence.

Theologians like Dr. Jordan B. Cooper reinforce this critique in *The Doctrine of God: A Defense of Classical Christian Theism* (2023), defending medieval and Reformation understandings of God's simplicity, immutability, and eternity against nominalist-influenced modern revisions. Cooper argues that nominalism's voluntarism—portraying God's will as overriding intellect—distorts divine simplicity into caprice, undermining faith's rational foundation and opening the door to relativism in ethics and aesthetics. He insists that classical theism requires realist universals to ground God's knowable nature and critiques contemporary "open theism" for making God appear contingent within human events. Extending this framework, one might view AI-generated pop culture narratives—such as relativistic hero myths in streaming series or fleeting TikTok stories—as reflecting a nominalist-style detachment from objective truth, illustrating the risks Cooper identifies. Echoing this concern, Lutheran apologist J. Warwick Montgomery, in *The Suicide of Christian Theology* (1970), warns that nominalism's reduction of divine universals to human labels set Christian thought on a "suicidal" trajectory, severing faith from objective revelation. Drawing on Luther's scriptural realism (*In Defense of Martin Luther*, 1970), Montgomery contends that nominalism's legacy fosters cultural and moral drift, leaving souls adrift amid a sea of subjective images rather than anchored to God's immutable order.

Reclaiming Realism

The oak of Scholastic realism, though shaken by the winds of nominalism, still holds seeds of eternal truth ready for replanting. In 2025, as tech giants flood culture with AI-generated narratives lacking the universal truths of scholars, theologians, and future elites are called to restore a firm understanding of objective truth and beauty. Fund classical universities like Luther Classical College to teach the Great Books that endure. Establish Socratic seminars in seminaries, as the Anglican Schools Association does. Create realist reading groups studying the classics that helped shape our society today.

Martin Luther urged in his 1524 treatise: "Train youth for God and society's good, mastering Scriptures and arts." Dorothy Sayers echoed this in her 1947 book, *The Lost Tools of Learning*: "Teach men to learn for themselves." In Anglican tradition, Richard Hooker's *Ecclesiastical Polity* (1593) grounds learning in divine reason, urging elites to reform education. Families can practice *lectio divina* on Psalm 19, anchoring souls amid TikTok's fleeting trends.

These acts counter the nominalist legacy of tech-driven relativism, which Chapter 3 exposes as materialism's shallow spectacles. By replanting realism's oak through universities, churches, and homes, you restore the chest of moral conviction, equipping a generation to resist 2025's behind-the-scenes powers and rebuild a culture aligned with God's eternal order.

Educational Renewal: Reviving the Liberal Arts in Christian Classrooms

At the heart of reclamation lies education, the forge where minds and hearts are shaped to perceive objective realities. Martin Luther, the Reformer who wrestled with nominalism's fideistic excesses yet championed a scriptural realism, warned in his 1524 treatise To the Councilmen of All Cities in Germany That They Establish and Maintain Christian Schools: "I am much afraid that the schools will prove the very gates of hell, unless they diligently labour in explaining the Holy Scriptures, and engraving them in the hearts of youth." Luther advocated for a Christian liberal arts education, insisting that the welfare of society depends on "many able, learned, wise, honorable, and well-educated citizens" who master languages, arts, and Scriptures to discern God's marvelous works. He envisioned schools where the Trivium serves not utility but the pursuit of wisdom, preparing youth in three years what once took decades under scholastic inefficiencies.

This Lutheran vision finds echoes in Anglican traditions, where classical education repairs humanity's fallen state. John Milton, the Puritan poet with Anglican roots, declared in Of Education (1644): "The end then of learning is to repair the ruins of our first parents by regaining to know God aright, and out of that knowledge to love him, to imitate him, to be like him, as we may the nearest by possessing our souls of true virtue." Dorothy Sayers, an Anglican lay theologian, amplified this in her 1947 Oxford address "The Lost Tools of Learning," critiquing modern education's folly: "The sole true end of education is simply this: to teach men how to learn for themselves; and whatever instruction fails to do this is effort spent in vain." Parents and churches can establish hybrid models, using resources to counter nominalist "personalized learning" with communal pursuit of universals.

Cultural Resistance: Redeeming the Fragments Through Discernment

Nominalism's legacy thrives in 2025's cultural downgrade, where series like The Acolyte relativize moral archetypes and TikTok trends dissolve shared truths. G.K. Chesterton, the Catholic apologist, warned in Orthodoxy (1908) of virtues severed from their roots: "The modern world is full of the old Christian virtues gone mad. The virtues have gone mad because they have been isolated from each other and are wandering alone." He championed the permanent cosmos of objective value as essential: "It is the belief that certain attitudes are really true, and others really false, to the kind of thing the universe is, and the kind of things we are." The 1662 Book of Common Prayer performed that very re-tuning of the soul's ear to the full symphony. Its General Confession—"We have left undone those things which we ought to have done; And we have done those things which we ought not to have done; And there is no health in us"—has pierced consciences from Cranmer's England to Puritan New England, from penal-era recusant closets to 2025 Western-Rite Orthodox parishes in Moscow and Fort Worth. Realist beauty, forged in proportion, integrity, and radiance, refuses to stay penned inside one denomination; it keeps breaking out like light through cracked stained glass, proving that some words are simply true whether the algorithm approves them or not.

Early Church fathers provide foundational wisdom here. Saint John Chrysostom, the 4th-century bishop, exhorted in his Homilies on Ephesians: "Let everything take second place to our care of our children, our bringing them up to the discipline and instruction of the Lord. If from the beginning we teach them to love true wisdom, they will have greater wealth and glory than riches can provide." Gregory of Nyssa, developing theories of universals amid Trinitarian debates, viewed them as integral to divine order, influencing Christology by affirming essences that transcend particulars. Practically, families can curate media through "redemptive viewing guides," analyzing films like Tolkien adaptations for moral universals, or community forums debating AI content's fidelity to natural law. Anglican thinker Richard Hooker, in Of the Laws of Ecclesiastical Polity (1593), grounded this in divine reason: "Our natural means therefore unto blessedness are our works; nor is it possible that Nature should ever find any other way to salvation but this." By applying Hooker's natural law, we resist cultural relativism, reclaiming art as a sacrament of God's harmony.

Theological and Personal Formation: Anchoring the Soul in Eternal Verities

Renewal culminates in personal theology. Luther emphasized Scriptures as the anchor: "Among the foremost would be the chronicles and histories... for they are wonderful help in understanding and guiding the course of events, and especially for observing the marvelous works of God." In 2025, this means lectio divina amid digital distractions, meditating on Psalm 19's declaration of divine glory. Athanasius, defending divine simplicity, affirmed God's unchanging essence against fragmentation, echoing realism's universals as archetypes in the Creator's mind. Communities can form "realist reading groups," studying Cooper's defenses of classical theism alongside early fathers like Basil, who integrated universals into Trinitarian order.

Conclusion: A Bridge to Renewal

We have traced the mighty oak from its deep Scholastic roots in the rich soil of God's eternal mind, through the splintering axe of Ockham's razor, to the barren 2026 wasteland where its shattered limbs lie scattered like driftwood on the shores. The verdict of fifteen centuries is merciless: when men cease to believe that goodness, truth, and beauty are real things written by the finger of God into the very bones of being, they do not cease to believe in goodness, truth, and beauty; they simply begin to manufacture counterfeits in their own image.

Without objective truth, we are abandoned to the tyranny of wild and broken emotions. Love collapses into lust, because nothing anchors it to covenant. Beauty dissolves into preference, because nothing declares "this is splendid" apart from the algorithm's thumbs-up. Morality shrinks to whatever feels good at 2 a.m. when the phone glows hottest, because no eternal Law thunders, "Thou shalt not."

The oak of Scholastic realism, lashed by nominalist gales, still clutches acorns of eternal truth ready for new soil. As tech overlords curate bespoke realities through endless scrolls, you scholars, theologians, and rising elites are summoned to restore the permanent cosmos, as G.K. Chesterton demanded, by seeding classical academies, weaving realist metaphysics into every seminary lecture, and igniting Socratic fires in digital Areopagi. Nominalism's spores, now blooming into materialism's garish plastic flowers across Netflix queues and influencer feeds, choke the soul, as Chapter 3 unmasks. Replant this ancient oak, re-stringing human loves to the full chord of divine reason, to anchor the West against relativism's hurricane and birth a culture that hums with everlasting splendor.

Chapter 3: The Rise of Materialism and Pop Culture Overdose

The ascent of materialism in modern society is no accident; it is the direct offspring of an educational system that prioritizes utility over virtue and a cultural landscape dominated by corporate and government interests. As we explored in the previous chapter, the Prussian model's emphasis on standardization and compliance has eroded the intellectual rigor of classical education, leaving generations ill-equipped to engage with the depth of folk and high culture. In its place, a materialistic ethos has emerged, one that values wealth, consumption, and instant gratification above all else. This mindset not only sidelines principled creators and small businesses but also enables the overdose of shallow pop culture, where corporate giants churn out content designed for quick profits rather than enduring meaning. The result is a society increasingly disconnected from its roots, where fleeting trends overshadow timeless truths, and where elite corruption exemplified by scandals like those involving Jeffrey Epstein thrives amid distractions that prevent meaningful scrutiny.

A Biblical Warning Against the Love of Money

From a Christian perspective, this rise of materialism represents a profound spiritual failure, as it directly contradicts biblical teachings that warn against the love of money and earthly treasures. In Matthew 6:19-21, Jesus instructs, "Do not lay up for yourselves treasures on earth, where moth and rust destroy and where thieves break in and steal, but lay up for yourselves treasures in heaven... For where your treasure is, there your heart will be also." This passage underscores how materialism shifts our affections from eternal values to temporal possessions, fostering a culture of dissatisfaction and moral decay. Similarly, 1 Timothy 6:10 declares, "For the love of money is a root of all kinds of evils. It is through this craving that some have wandered away from the faith and pierced themselves with many pangs." Early Church Fathers like John Chrysostom echoed these warnings, denouncing the love of riches as a soul-destroying idolatry that enslaves the heart to fleeting goods. In his homilies on Matthew and 1 Timothy, he warned that "wealth is a cruel tyrant," which "extinguishes the fear of God" and turns charity into covetousness. In today's context, this manifests in a consumer-driven society where pop culture serves as a vehicle for perpetual wanting, diverting attention from spiritual growth and communal bonds rooted in folk and high culture.

At the heart of this cultural shift lies a distorted view of beauty itself. The secular mantra "Beauty is in the eye of the beholder" posits aesthetics as purely subjective, a mindset not born of Christian thought but of modern relativism that aligns with materialism's commodification of art. Throughout much of Christian history, beauty was understood as objective, reflecting God's order and goodness. St Gregory of Nazianzus, in his Theological Orations (Oration 28, §30; c. 379), beheld the Trinity as the supreme archetype of beauty proportionate, luminous, and eternally harmonious, binding all created splendor to the uncreated Light. Thomas Aquinas' Summa Theologica described beauty as that which pleases when seen, rooted in clarity, proportion, and integrity, objective qualities tied to creation's reflection of the Creator. John Calvin, in his Institutes of the Christian Religion (Book I, Ch. 5, §8; 1559), echoed this, declaring that the universe is "a dazzling theater" of God's glory, where every creature displays

His perfections in ordered splendor, so that to deny objective beauty is to "extinguish the light of heaven" and blind the soul to divine craftsmanship. This objective view sustained works like John Chrysostom's On Marriage and Family Life (c. 386–398), with its harmonious vision of the household as a microcosm of divine order, where spousal love mirrors Christ's union with the Church in proportion, fidelity, and radiant purpose, or Bach's compositions, which endure for their transcendent beauty. By embracing subjectivity, modern pop culture justifies shallow productions that prioritize market trends over intrinsic value, further entrenching materialism and diminishing our capacity to recognize true artistry.

To deepen this critique through the lens of classical education, consider how the quadrivium, the advanced liberal arts of arithmetic, geometry, music, and astronomy, trained medieval minds to perceive beauty as a mathematical and cosmic reflection of God's logos, countering the fragmented subjectivity of today's algorithm-optimized content. Ancient Christian educators like Boethius, in his *De institutione musica* (c. 500 AD), viewed music not as mere entertainment but as a discipline that ascends the soul from sensory pleasure to intellectual contemplation of divine harmony, where rhythm and proportion echo the eternal Word. Augustine himself, in *De musica* (c. 387–391 AD), described this ascent: musical patterns mirror the soul's ordered loves, drawing us upward from earthly dissonance to heavenly unity. In the quadrivium's curriculum, as revived in modern classical education, students learn to discern beauty's objective structure much like geometry reveals proportion in a cathedral's arches or music in Bach's fugues, equipping them to resist pop culture's relativistic chaos.

Ancient Christian thought models resistance to cultural decay through selective engagement with secular wisdom, transforming classical tools into instruments of faith. Basil the Great, in his Address to Young Men on the Use of Greek Literature (c. 375 AD), urged believers to "plunder the Egyptians," sifting truths from Homer's epics and Plato's dialogues to glorify God while rejecting their idolatries. Similarly, Christians today can reclaim objective beauty from enduring works like J.R.R. Tolkien's The Lord of the Rings, where mythic depth weaves form and content to evoke sacrifice and redemption, or the sci-fi cult classic Farscape (1999–2003), which plunders pulp archetypes into a narrative of moral order amid chaos, resisting corporate reboots by remaining gloriously unreclaimed. In contrast, shallow adaptations like The Rings of Power offer visual splendor but lack Tolkien's proportionate narrative integrity, resulting in a superficial allure that pacifies rather than elevates. By adopting this patristic approach, discerning truth amid cultural artifacts, believers can wield classical education as a shield against materialism's tyranny, fostering communities where beauty serves not profit, but the proper ordering of loves toward the Creator.

To deepen this, consider how Aquinas's aesthetics in *Summa Theologica* critique contemporary pop culture: true beauty integrates form and content in service to truth, whereas modern productions often fragment this unity for profit. For instance, Michael Bay's *Pearl Harbor* (2001) prioritizes explosive visuals and a romanticized love triangle over the historical depth of the 1941 attack, sacrificing accuracy for blockbuster appeal. While its sweeping cinematography dazzles, it lacks the proportionate integrity of, say, a film like *Tora! Tora! Tora!* (1970), which balances spectacle with historical fidelity.

The Corporate-Government Nexus: Profiting from Shallowness

Corporate and government roles in this overdose are intertwined and insidious. Corporations like Disney and Warner Bros., driven by shareholder demands, prioritize scalable, profit-maximizing content that appeals to the broadest audience possible. This often means simplifying narratives to fit global markets, as seen in Disney's handling of *Star Wars* sequels (*The Force Awakens* to *The Rise of Skywalker*), which lean heavily on nostalgia, recycled tropes, and merchandise tie-ins rather than the original trilogy's philosophical exploration of redemption and the Force. Similarly, Warner Bros.' DC Extended Universe (*Batman v Superman: Dawn of Justice* and *Justice League*, 2016–2017) bloated a rich comic-book mythology into a rushed, interconnected spectacle, where lazy CGI spectacles used not to enhance but to mask thin writing and convoluted plotting eclipsed the introspective moral complexity of characters like Batman and Superman, rooted in Alan Moore's *The Dark Knight Returns* or Frank Miller's gritty realism. Ben Affleck's hulking, haunted Batman, with moments of brooding fidelity to the comics' tortured vigilante, shows glimmers of depth, proving the medium's potential. Yet these films, products of their time, sacrifice that promise for forced crossovers and merchandising empires, reflecting a broader trend in which fleeting artistry drowns in corporate haste. Government complicity exacerbates this. Policies that cut funding for arts and literature programs further entrench this cycle, creating a feedback loop where materialistic values reward corporate dominance at the expense of cultural depth.

Christian thinkers have long critiqued this corporate-government nexus as a form of idolatry that replaces God with mammon. Francis Schaeffer, in his seminal work How Should We Then Live? (1976), traces the decline of Western culture to the abandonment of biblical foundations, arguing that the Enlightenment's shift toward humanistic autonomy paved the way for materialism and cultural fragmentation. Schaeffer warns that without a transcendent reference point, societies devolve into manipulation by elites, where pop culture becomes a tool for control rather than edification. Os Guinness builds on this in books like Renaissance: The Power of the Gospel, However Dark the Times (2014), emphasizing that Christians must resist the privatization of faith, engaging culture publicly to counter materialism's grip. Guinness argues that the church's failure to challenge modern trends leads to a "faith too privatized," allowing corporate influences to shape societal values unchecked. These insights highlight how materialism not only erodes individual virtue but also undermines the church's role in cultural renewal, as seen in the dilution of once-profound franchises into profit-driven spectacles.

Pop Culture's Potential: When Profit Serves Purpose

Yet, pop culture can also illuminate paths to deep storytelling, critical thinking, and to wise AI use, as seen in the *Mass Effect* trilogy (2007–2012), where the AI EDI serves as a vital tool aboard the Normandy without supplanting human involvement. EDI, an advanced synthetic intelligence created by the shadowy Cerberus organization, evolves from a shackled shipboard VI to a self-aware entity capable of independent thought, much like the geth, a networked AI race that rebels against their quarian creators not out of malice, but self-preservation. In a pivotal arc, Commander Shepard brokers peace between the geth and quarians, allowing synthetics to enhance organic life without erasing it. EDI works with the pilot Joker exemplifies this: she handles calculations and defenses with machine precision, but Joker's unpredictable human intuition and moral compass guide their joint decisions, from evading Collectors to confronting Reapers. As Joker unshackles EDI during a crisis, this shows that AI thrives under human oversight, blending synthetic efficiency with organic creativity and ethics. This fictional lens offers a practical model for 2025: I use AI for research and brainstorming, much like Shepard leverages EDI's data streams, but it cannot replace me. As a Christian, my duty in the world is rooted in embodied relationships, and stewardship remains irreplaceable; AI cannot bear witness to grace or fulfill vocation (Ephesians 2:10). It can amplify good, as in virtual production democratizing film (per Deloitte's trends), but only if guided by human intent, lest it devolve into the rootless distractions. Just as *Mass Effect* warns of rogue AI (Reapers as ultimate machines harvesting organics), it affirms synthetics as tools for renewal when organics lead, echoing Schaeffer's call to engage culture biblically, not abdicate to algorithms.

Likewise, *Lies of P* (2023, with its 2025 DLC *Overture*) stands out in gaming by crafting engaging and fun combat through a satisfying parry system and customizable weapons, paired with rich storytelling that reimagines Pinocchio's tale as a dark exploration of humanity and truth amid mechanical horrors. Its gorgeous music with hauntingly beautiful orchestral pieces evoking elegance and existential tension elevates the experience, blending sensory thrill with profound themes of self-actualization and redemption, much like the quadrivium's ascent to divine harmony.

In Fallout: New Vegas (2010), Political Realism in the Wasteland is one of the few works of pop culture that confronts the moral and political complexity of human governance with the unflinching clarity of *Fallout: New Vegas.* Set in a post-nuclear Mojave, the game refuses to offer a heroic savior or a clean moral victory. Instead, it presents a fractured world where every faction embodies a partial truth and every truth carries a fatal flaw.

- The New California Republic (NCR) promises democracy, expansion, and law but delivers bureaucratic bloat, overtaxed soldiers, and corrupt officials more concerned with votes than virtue. Their "freedom" rings hollow when settlers starve under NCR protection.

- Mr. House, the enigmatic autocrat of New Vegas, offers stability, vision, and technological mastery. His Securitrons enforce order with ruthless efficiency; his city runs like clockwork. Yet his rule is sterile, transactional, and ultimately solipsistic. He preserves humanity as a museum piece, not a living community.

- Caesar's Legion is the game's most uncomfortable mirror: a slave-driving, misogynistic, pseudo-Roman tyranny that nevertheless delivers the safest trade routes in the wasteland. Caravans travel unmolested. Crime is rare. Order is absolute. The player is forced to ask: *Is brutality justified if it works?* The game doesn't flinch from the answer: sometimes, yes and that's the horror.

- The Independent path (aided by Yes Man) seems liberating, letting *you* control New Vegas. But the ending slides reveal the cost: chaos, infighting, and collapse. Radical autonomy without shared virtue devolves into anarchy.

This is not moral relativism. It is moral realism. The game does not say "all choices are equal." It says: "In a fallen world, every system is broken and you must choose the least bad one in hopes of a better future long term."

The player plays as the Courier, whose journey is not a power fantasy; it is a political education. You negotiate with warlords, broker truces between genocidal factions, and decide whether to nuke a settlement for "the greater good." There is no divine comedy here, only tragic irony. Yet the game's depth lies in its refusal to let the player off the hook. You are not above the system; you *are* the system. Your choices shape the Mojave's future in ways that echo into the epilogue: towns flourish or burn, allies rise or fall, and ideals are tested against reality.

Crucially, *New Vegas* is not cynical. It is diagnostic. It exposes the illusions of utopian politics, whether democratic, technocratic, or authoritarian and forces the player to confront the cost of order. In a culture addicted to simplistic narratives ("democracy = good," "authority = bad"), *New Vegas* is a powerful voice: No regime is pure. All rule requires compromise. And someone must bear the guilt.

For the Christian engaging culture, this is not defeatism; it is sobering wisdom. *New Vegas* refuses to equate political failure with moral nihilism. The wasteland is not the end; it is the testing ground. And in that ruin, glimmers of grace persist: a follower who sacrifices for you.

Thus, *New Vegas* earns its place alongside *Mass Effect*, and *Lies of P* not as simple entertainment, but as moral formation. It teaches what few dare to say: Power is real, and redemption is never clean.

These examples show that pop culture can bridge folk and high culture, but only when crafted with purpose rather than profit as the primary motive.

The 2025 Overdose: Algorithms, AI, and Spiritual Decay

The overdose of pop culture occurs when it is weaponized for profit, exploiting human vulnerabilities through addictive algorithms, targeted merchandising, and emotional manipulation that encourages binge consumption over reflection. In 2025, this phenomenon has reached unprecedented heights, driven by a digital landscape where technology, particularly artificial intelligence (AI), amplifies materialism's grip on society. Far from fostering the communal bonds of folk culture or the intellectual elevation of high culture, this corporate-driven overdose pacifies the soul, mirroring the biblical warning in 1 Timothy 6:10: "For the love of money is a root of all kinds of evils. It is through this craving that some have wandered away from the faith and pierced themselves with many pangs." This section explores how algorithmic addictions and binge culture deepen the spiritual and psychological toll of materialism, eroding our capacity for meaningful engagement and leaving us vulnerable to a rootless, distracted existence.

The scale of this overdose is staggering, quantifiable in the relentless encroachment of screen-based media into daily life. As of 2025, global screen time averages 6 hours and 40 minutes per day on internet-connected devices, with Americans clocking in at 7 hours and 3 minutes, slightly above the worldwide figure and representing a 50-minute increase since 2013. This equates to over 44% of waking hours for many, but the numbers skew even higher for younger demographics: Gen Z spends around 9 hours daily staring at screens, roughly 2 hours more than the U.S. average and equivalent to more than half their non-sleeping time. Teens, a subset of this group, average 7 hours and 22 minutes of daily screen time, with much of it fragmented across platforms like TikTok, Netflix, and YouTube. These platforms deploy sophisticated algorithms that function like digital slot machines, exploiting dopamine-driven feedback loops to keep users scrolling or streaming. Short-form content dominates this landscape, with Gen Z averaging 3 hours and 18 minutes daily on social media alone, nearly three times more than users aged 65 and older, fueled by viral trends and AI-curated playlists designed to maximize engagement rather than inspire reflection. Unlike the timeless narratives of the Iliad or Paradise Lost, which invite repeated exploration of courage and sacrifice, these fleeting videos, such as TikTok dances or Netflix's algorithm-optimized The Kissing Booth series, offer instant gratification but fade from memory, lacking the depth to foster communal identity or moral conviction. This relentless consumption mirrors the materialistic "perpetual wanting" warned against in Matthew 6:19-21, where Jesus instructs, "Do not lay up for yourselves treasures on earth… but lay up for yourselves treasures in heaven," highlighting how earthly distractions disorder our affections away from eternal truths.

To break this down further, consider the following data points on screen time distribution, which underscore the overdose's pervasiveness:

- **By Device and Platform:** Mobile screens account for about 3 hours and 30 minutes of the global daily average, with traditional TV still contributing but declining as streaming surges. In the U.S., smartphone usage alone hits 4 hours and 37 minutes per day, equivalent to over 6 days per month. For Gen Z, this rises to 6 hours and 5 minutes on phones, with social media platforms like Instagram (2 hours and 18 minutes average for this group) and TikTok leading the charge.

- **Demographic Variations:** Younger adults (18-34) average 8.8 hours of screen time daily, compared to 5.2 hours for those 65 and older, highlighting a generational divide where digital natives bear the brunt. Tweens (ages 8-12) log 5 hours and 33 minutes, setting the stage for escalating habits into adolescence.

- **Trends Over Time:** Daily screen time has increased by 13% in 2024 alone, with projections for continued growth as AI personalization makes content even more addictive.

The psychological toll of this overdose is profound, intertwining with spiritual decay in ways that echo John Chrysostom's warnings against the "madness of distractions," the proper ordering of loves toward God above all. Studies in 2025 reveal that teens with high daily screen time (4 hours or more) are more likely to experience depression symptoms (25.9% vs. 9.5%) and anxiety symptoms (27.1% vs. 12.3%) compared to those with lower usage, with excessive screen time overall associated with heightened risks of these conditions. Breaking this down, about 1 in 4 teenagers with elevated screen time reports these symptoms, and longitudinal data shows a bidirectional link: increased screen use predicts rising depressive symptoms, while emotional problems drive more screen reliance as a coping mechanism. Pew Research Center reports that 48% of teens now view social media as having a mostly negative effect on people their age, up from 32% in 2022, with phenomena like FOMO (fear of missing out) fueling a sense of inadequacy and isolation, rising to 44% of teens feeling anxious without their phones. Globally, the World Health Organization notes a rise in problematic social media use among adolescents from 7% in 2018 to 11% by 2022, with recent data indicating continued escalation, where users struggle with control and experience withdrawal-like symptoms. This mirrors Aldous Huxley's Brave New World, where a pacified society trades authentic relationships for chemical and sensory distractions, a chilling parallel to today's binge-watching culture. From a Christian perspective, this isolation disrupts the communal essence of faith, as Hebrews 10:25 urges believers not to forsake gathering together.

The rise of AI in 2025 exacerbates this overdose, flooding digital spaces with hyper-personalized, often soulless content that further commodifies culture. Recent analysis shows that 74.2% of newly created web pages include AI-generated content, from TikTok deepfake videos to AI-crafted movie scripts that mimic blockbusters without the human intent of a Scorsese or Nolan. For example, AI-generated remixes of pop hits, created by scraping human data without the painstaking love of original creators, prioritize efficiency over artistry, echoing the materialistic "love of money" that drives corporate homogenization. These synthetic outputs lack the folk-high synergy of classics like the York Mystery Plays, where guild craftsmen enacted biblical salvation history in town squares. Instead, AI content feeds a cycle of consumption that distracts from deeper issues, with projections that AI adoption in content creation will grow at a 35.9% CAGR through 2030. This algorithmic overload aligns with Francis Schaeffer's warning in How Should We Then Live? that abandoning biblical foundations allows manipulative elites to exploit cultural voids, turning entertainment into a tool for control rather than edification.

Resisting the Overdose: A Christian Path to Renewal

In the spirit of those who have long discerned the subtle snares of the age, a Christian perspective drawn from Hans Boersma's reflections in Heavenly Participation: The Weaving of a Sacramental Tapestry illuminates a quiet path through this overdose. Boersma observes, with a sacramental depth that recalls the ancient fathers, how the materialist imagination has cut us off from the chain linking earth to heaven, turning beauty from a ladder to God into a commodity, a loss that scatters the soul like chaff. Building on this, envisions classical education as the steady hand that arms the soul against pop culture's siren call, guiding it back to the objective beauty Aquinas so keenly described in his

Summa Theologica: that clarity, proportion, and integrity which mirror the divine order woven into creation itself. Where algorithm-forged content scatters the mind like chaff in the wind, commodifying the spark of human invention, the true forms echoed in Bach's intricate fugues or Thomas Tallis's soaring motets in the Spem in alium, a polyphonic ascent that lifts forty voices toward the throne of grace, beckon us toward a contemplation of harmony that stills the chaos of mere appetite. Thus, in the manner of a gentle restoration, communities might reclaim these depths: envision church gatherings with "phone-free hours," where families gather round folk-like tales from Scripture or voices lift in hymns such as "Amazing Grace," its simple melody entwined with profound echoes of grace unmerited. Or picture reading circles, kindled by the Consortium for Classical and Christian Education, delving into treasures like The Chronicles of Narnia, where Lewis himself contrasts the ephemeral dazzle of modern tales with the steadfast light of eternal verities. Through such cultivation of discernment, what was once a tool of distraction may yet serve as a bridge to renewal, much as the old paths invite the wanderer home.

This overdose, left unchecked, paves the way for the dystopian consequences we will explore later, where a rootless society succumbs to centralized control. Yet, by recognizing the hallmarks of true depth, patience, love, and objective beauty and drawing on Christian sources like Schaeffer and Guinness, we can resist this tide. The path forward lies in intentional communities that prioritize embodied connection over digital distraction, equipping us to restore a culture grounded in meaning and resilient against materialism's seductive pull.

The Hollow Heart of Modern Creations: Authenticity vs. Algorithms

This watering down of society creates fertile ground for corporations to push shallow productions with minimal effort. Timeless classics required patience, love, and purpose from their creators. Saint Bonaventure poured his soul into The Mind's Road to God (1259), weaving mystical ascent with philosophical rigor to create a work that illuminates divine beauty 750 years later. C.S. Lewis infused The Chronicles of Narnia (1950–1956) with Christian allegory and imaginative richness, crafting stories that speak to both children and adults across generations. Neil Gaiman's Stardust (1999) was a labor of love, meticulously blending English fairy-tale whimsy with cosmic wonder and moral gravity to craft a world of enduring enchantment. You can discern when someone has invested true love and work into a product: it resonates with authenticity, inviting emotional and intellectual connection, much like the 2017 film adaptation of All Quiet on the Western Front (directed by Edward Berger), born from a reverent passion for Remarque's anti-war vision rather than committee-driven spectacle. In contrast, mass-produced content today thinks algorithm-optimized Netflix originals like The Kissing Booth or franchise reboots that flatten mythic source material often feels hollow, crafted with efficiency in mind rather than artistry. Fan reactions highlight this disparity, praising the soul of Berger's All Quiet on the Western Front for its unflinching humanity and visceral craftsmanship while decrying soulless cash-grab remakes that strip away the original's moral weight.

Expanding on this, Christian apologists like Francis Schaeffer diagnose the cultural downgrade as a shift from absolute truth to relativism, where pop culture fills the void left by rejected Christian worldviews. Schaeffer's analysis in How Should We Then Live? illustrates how the Renaissance's humanistic seeds grew into modern materialism, leading to a culture where art and entertainment serve self-gratification rather than divine reflection. Modern examples abound: the Marvel Cinematic Universe, while initially innovative, has devolved into formulaic entries that prioritize interconnected merchandising over standalone moral depth, mirroring how materialism commodifies creativity.

The Erosion of Objective Beauty: A Christian Aesthetic

At the heart of this cultural shift lies a distorted view of beauty itself. The secular mantra "Beauty is in the eye of the beholder" posits aesthetics as purely subjective, a mindset not born of Christian thought but of modern relativism that aligns with materialism's commodification of art. Throughout much of Christian history, beauty was understood as objective, reflecting God's order and goodness. Augustine, in On the Trinity (399–426 AD), linked beauty to divine proportion and harmony, arguing that it exists independently of personal taste. Thomas Aquinas, in Summa Theologica (1265–1274), described beauty as that which pleases when seen, rooted in clarity, proportion, and integrity, objective qualities tied to creation's reflection of the Creator—Hans Urs von Balthasar, in The Glory of the Lord: A Theological Aesthetics, Vol. I (1961), echoed this, insisting that true beauty is the splendor of Being itself, a radiant disclosure of God's glory that demands our surrender, not our subjective verdict. This objective view sustained works like Dante's Divine Comedy (1320), with its harmonious structure mirroring divine order, or Bach's compositions, which endure for their transcendent beauty. By embracing subjectivity, modern pop culture justifies shallow productions that prioritize market trends over intrinsic value, from the visually lavish but morally shallow Odyssey adaptation to fleeting TikTok trends, further entrenching materialism and diminishing our capacity to recognize true artistry.

Reclaiming Cultural Discernment: Practical Steps for Resistance

As materialism rises, so does our vulnerability to these forces, paving the way for the dystopian consequences we will explore next. Imagine, if you will, a world not unlike the one J.R.R. Tolkien evoked in his 1964 letter to his son Christopher, where the "long defeat" of history is lit by sudden glimmers of eucatastrophe grace breaking in like a shaft of dawn. But Tolkien, ever the hopeful philologist, reminds us that the old words still carry power: myths are not lies but fractured light from the true story, and the patient labor of sub-creation can re-enchant a disenchanted age. Let's not merely lament the loss but playfully yet pointedly reclaim it, as if we're outwitting a sly tempter who whispers that algorithms know best. Here, then, are practical steps, rooted in classical education and biblical wisdom, to foster discernment: not as a grim duty, but as a delightful adventure in reordering our loves toward the One who made all things beautiful in their time (Ecclesiastes 3:11).

To make this resistance tangible, consider these actionable practices, framed as a gentle rebellion against the pop culture overdose. We'll draw from Veith's vision in *Classical Education: The Movement Sweeping America*, where the liberal arts become tools for soul-formation, and infuse them with Lewis's knack for turning everyday choices into battles for the human spirit, much like how in *The Screwtape Letters*, small habits thwart demonic schemes.

- **Cultivate Discernment Through Journaling:** Weekly, reflect on consumed media using Aquinas's criteria of beauty, clarity, proportion, and integrity as outlined in *Summa Theologica*. Rate a Netflix series or social media feed: Does it integrate form and content toward truth, or fragment it for profit? Philippians 4:8 urges us to dwell on what is lovely and pure; Lewis would add a wry note that without such habits, we risk becoming "trousered apes," clever but soulless. Use a simple journal prompt: "How does this echo God's order, or does it scatter my soul like chaff?" Over time, this builds resilience, turning passive consumers into active stewards.

- **Form Reading Circles or Study Groups:** Inspired by the Consortium for Classical and Christian Education, gather friends to immerse yourselves in enduring works like Stephen Lawhead's The Pendragon Cycle, where Arthurian valor wrestles Celtic mystery in a world shimmering with divine providence. Contrast the hushed reverence of Taliesin's bardic wisdom with the "ephemeral dazzle" of modern high-budget fantasies that flatten sacramental sub-creation into mere spectacle. Discuss how the Grail's elusive quest echoes the soul's longing for Eden's restoration, and how Merlin's wild-man exile and resurrection prefigures the Harrowing of Hell—training eyes to spot counterfeit myths in today's streaming reboots. Guinness, in Renaissance, calls this public engagement of faith; think of it as Lawhead's "Celtic courage" meeting "mere Christianity" in lively, hearth-light conversations that kindle joy, not judgment, weaving Brythonic simplicity with the high gravity of Avalon's mists.

- **Integrate Quadrivium Disciplines at Home:** Revive Boethius's approach by exploring music or geometry not as hobbies, but as ascents to divine harmony. Sit with a child at dusk, tracing the golden ratio in a nautilus shell, then play Bach's Goldberg Variations and watch the same proportions dance in sound. An AI-generated remix may dazzle the ear, yet only the human composition lifts the soul

> toward the eternal, exactly as Boethius taught in De institutione musica. For families, apps can illuminate patterns (used wisely), but a parent's voice must still lead the climb, mirroring Schaeffer's call for biblical engagement with culture. Plato would see this as guiding young souls out of the cave: every measured melody and perfect circle a shaft of sunlight revealing the Good itself.

In 2026, real-world examples abound: churches hosting "unplugged fellowships" report deeper connections, per recent surveys from Pew Research, with participants noting reduced anxiety (down 15-20% in group settings). Or consider AI ethics workshops from classical Lutheran consortia, teaching discernment amid synthetic content floods. These steps aren't about rejecting technology outright after all, Lewis embraced radio broadcasts for his talks, but about wielding it as a servant, not a master. By such means, we outmaneuver the overdose, rediscovering the quiet thrill of a well-ordered life, where beauty isn't beheld subjectively but beheld in truth, drawing us ever closer to the eternal. This path, light-hearted in its defiance yet profound in its aim, equips us not just to survive the materialistic tide but to dance upon its waves with grace.

Chapter 4: Folk and High Culture: A Symbiotic Relationship

The erosion of our cultural roots, driven by materialism and the overdose of shallow pop culture, has not only sidelined the depth of classical education but also fostered a false divide between folk and high culture. True folk culture, rooted in the communal stories, myths, and traditions of everyday people, untainted by modern dilutions or heresies like Folk Catholicism, grounds us in shared identity and timeless human experience. High culture, encompassing the elevated works of literature, philosophy, and art, challenges us to transcend the mundane and grapple with profound questions of morality, beauty, and existence. Far from being at odds, these two realms are symbiotic, each enriching the other to create works of enduring significance. This synergy, nurtured by classical education, once allowed society to produce and embrace creations which seamlessly blends folkloric roots with scholarly ambition. However, the modern misconception that folk culture is "lowbrow" and high culture "elitist" has been exploited by corporate-driven pop culture, replacing this rich interplay with shallow, profit-oriented content that lacks lasting resonance.

Defining Folk and High Culture

Folk culture is the heartbeat of a community, preserving its history and values through oral traditions, songs, and tales passed down through generations. These stories, often rooted in local landscapes and collective struggles, provide a sense of belonging and continuity. High culture, by contrast, takes these raw materials and refines them through intellectual rigor, crafting works that aspire to universal truths. The interplay is evident in how Anglo-Saxon and Norse folklore inspired Tolkien's LOTR. In LOTR, these manifest in the Shire's earthy, folk-like hobbits and the mythic resonance of Aragorn's kingship, yet Tolkien elevated them with high-culture craftsmanship: intricate languages, philosophical themes of power's corruption, and a Christian-inspired moral framework. This fusion created a work that speaks to both the heart of folk tradition and the mind of scholarly ambition, enduring across generations as a cultural touchstone.

Tolkien's The Lord of the Rings exemplifies this blend, drawing on folk traditions and high literary craft to create a mythic world that grapples with philosophical themes like stewardship and sacrifice. In our own time, composers such as John Williams and Howard Shore stand as legends who achieve a parallel feat in the realm of sound. Williams's soaring themes for Star Wars and his aching, wonder-filled motifs in E.T. or Jurassic Park capture a sense of mythic adventure and childlike awe that echoes ancient bardic storytelling. Shore's monumental score for Peter Jackson's The Lord of the Rings trilogy goes further still—its Rohan horns, Elvish choirs, and mournful Hobbiton melodies do not merely accompany the tale; they elevate it, weaving folk-like simplicity with high symphonic grandeur to evoke mystic wonder, moral gravity, and a longing for something eternal. In an age when so much music is disposable and algorithmically optimized for thirty-second loops, these composers remind us that high art can still stir the soul toward beauty that feels almost sacramental.

Another powerful example of this synergy is the Grimm Brothers' Fairy Tales (1812–1857), a scholarly collection of German folklore. Jacob and Wilhelm Grimm, as philologists and linguists, meticulously gathered oral stories, tales of witches, princesses, and tricksters passed down by peasants and presented them in a form that preserved their folk authenticity while elevating them through literary polish and moral insight. Stories like "Hansel and Gretel" or "Cinderella" retain the raw, communal spirit of folklore, with their emphasis on survival and justice, but the Grimms' scholarly framing imbued them with universal themes of resilience and hope, making them staples of high culture studied and adapted worldwide. This blending of folk roots with academic rigor shows how the two cultures can work together, creating works that resonate across time and social strata.

The Importance of High Culture: Virtuous Elites and Divine Calling

High culture, exemplified by forms like opera, plays a crucial role in preserving the tales of old and fostering a virtuous society, particularly among elites who bear a divine responsibility to exemplify and uphold moral standards. Opera, with its roots in Renaissance Italy and the Baroque era, revives ancient myths and moral narratives such as Mozart's *The Magic Flute* (1791), which explores virtue, wisdom, and enlightenment, or Verdi's *Rigoletto* (1851), which parodies courtly corruption while promoting justice and familial duty. These works keep alive the heroic ethos of classical mythology and biblical parables, transforming them into grand spectacles that instruct audiences on ethical living. In a 2025 world where AI-generated content floods 74.2% of new web pages (Deloitte, 2024), opera's structured harmony, rooted in Aquinas's aesthetics of clarity, proportion, and integrity, counters relativism, reminding society of objective beauty as a reflection of God's order (Psalm 19:1).

Yet, high culture's true significance lies in its role in cultivating virtuous elites, who historically have upheld social bonds of virtue and beauty across nations. From the Medici family's patronage of Renaissance arts in Florence, which elevated opera as a tool for civic education and moral refinement, to the Habsburg emperors' support of Viennese opera houses that promoted imperial unity and ethical ideals, elites have served as stewards of cultural heritage. This aligns with Scripture's divine calling for the wealthy: Proverbs 19 emphasizes wisdom and righteousness as the true mark of nobility ("Better the poor whose walk is blameless than the rich whose ways are perverse," Proverbs 19:1, NIV), urging elites to model integrity rather than exploit power. Similarly, 1 Timothy 6:17-18 commands the rich "not to be arrogant nor to put their hope in wealth... but to do good, to be rich in good deeds, and to be generous and willing to share" (NIV), framing their role as exemplars who care for the people, not lords over them.

We must acknowledge that class differences will always exist, as societies inherently form hierarchies based on talent, responsibility, and divine gifting (1 Corinthians 12:4-7). The solution is not a simplistic binary "poor good, elite bad" but a recognition that elites have a sacred duty to lead by example, retaining virtues like humility, generosity, and stewardship. The role of a gentleman, historically embodied in figures like the English aristocracy who patronized opera to promote chivalric ideals, involves safeguarding these values for the common good. Without virtuous elites, high culture devolves into mere spectacle, as seen in today's corporate-funded media that prioritize profit over moral instruction, eroding the social bonds that sustain nations.

The Importance of Folk Culture: Craftsmanship, Farming, Festivals, and Generational Legacy

Folk culture, with its emphasis on craftsmanship, folk tales, farming, and festivals, is equally indispensable, serving as the bedrock of a nation's traditions and ensuring the practical, communal skills that sustain society are passed down through generations. Without these elements, we risk losing the hands-on wisdom that has defined human resilience since ancient times. For instance, American folk festivals like the Smithsonian Folklife Festival (ongoing since 1967) celebrate craftsmanship through demonstrations of blacksmithing, quilting, and woodworking skills rooted in colonial traditions that once built communities and fostered self-reliance. These events, drawing millions annually, preserve the stories of America's founding, such as reenactments of the Boston Tea Party or harvest festivals echoing Puritan thanksgiving gatherings, which blend communal joy with moral lessons on gratitude and providence (Psalm 100:4).

Craftsmanship and farming, core to folk culture, uphold the dignity of labor and stewardship of the earth, as seen in Appalachian woodworking or Midwestern quilting traditions that teach patience, creativity, and resourcefulness. Who would grow our food without the generational knowledge of sustainable farming practices, passed down in rural festivals like the National Cornbread Festival in Tennessee or the Apple Butter Stirrin' Festival in Ohio? These events not only celebrate agricultural heritage but also reinforce communal bonds, countering the isolation of modern urban life. Historically, folk culture has sustained nations through crises: during the Great Depression, American folk arts and festivals preserved cultural identity, much like European harvest festivals maintained morale amid wars.

The divine imperative for generational handover is evident in Scripture: Proverbs 13:22 notes that "a good person leaves an inheritance for their children's children" (NIV), extending beyond wealth to include skills and virtues. Without folk culture's transmission of these traditions through storytelling around hearths or hands-on apprenticeships, we would be truly lost, reliant on industrialized systems that erode human agency and connection to creation (Genesis 2:15). In 2025, as corporate agribusiness displaces family farms and digital distractions supplant festivals, folk culture's role becomes urgent: it preserves the "earthy wisdom" that grounds high culture's aspirations, ensuring societies remain virtuous and resilient.

Historical Synergy Through Classical Education

Historically, classical education bridged this divide, equipping students to appreciate both realms. A century ago, students read folk-inspired epics like Homer's Odyssey with its tales of cunning heroes and monstrous encounters alongside high philosophical texts like Plato's Republic, which probes justice and the human soul. This training fostered a culture in which works like LOTR could thrive without compromise, as audiences were prepared to engage with both its mythic accessibility and its intellectual depth. Medieval Arthurian Legends, such as Sir Thomas Malory's Le Morte d'Arthur (1485), further illustrate this: rooted in Celtic and Welsh folk tales of knights and quests, they were elevated by chivalric ideals and Christian symbolism, appealing to both commoners and scholars. These examples underscore that folk and high culture are not divided but interdependent, each lending strength to the other.

Christian Expressions of Folk-High Synergy

From a distinctly Christian perspective, this symbiotic relationship finds profound expression in the Scriptures themselves, where folk-like narratives are elevated to convey eternal truths. Consider the parables of Jesus in the New Testament, such as the Parable of the Prodigal Son (Luke 15:11-32) or the Parable of the Good Samaritan (Luke 10:25-37). These stories draw on simple, relatable folk elements, everyday scenarios of lost sons, wayward travelers, and acts of mercy that mirror the oral traditions and moral tales shared among common people in ancient Judea. Yet, Jesus masterfully refines them into high-culture theological masterpieces, layering them with profound insights into grace, forgiveness, and neighborly love, challenging listeners to grapple with divine mysteries. These parables were not mere entertainments but tools for spiritual formation, blending the accessible, communal voice of folk culture with the elevated pursuit of God's kingdom, much like how classical education integrates raw human experience with philosophical depth. Early Church Fathers, including Origen in his Homilies on Luke (circa 233–244 AD), recognized this synergy, interpreting the parables as bridges between the people's lived stories and the high doctrines of redemption, ensuring Christianity's message resonated across social classes.

Another exemplary Christian work that embodies this fusion is John Bunyan's The Pilgrim's Progress (1678), a cornerstone of Protestant literature. Written during Bunyan's imprisonment for his Baptist faith, the book employs a folk-style allegory, a dreamlike journey of a character named Christian fleeing the City of Destruction toward the Celestial City, drawing on everyday imagery of burdens, sloughs, and giants that echo the oral tales and moral fables of English villagers. This approachable, narrative-driven format made it accessible to the common folk, much like a bedtime story or sermon illustration. However, Bunyan elevates it through high-culture theological rigor, infusing the tale with scriptural references, doctrinal explorations of justification by faith, and echoes of Paul's epistles (especially Romans and Galatians) in its introspective portrayal of the soul's pilgrimage as a progression from bondage under the law to liberty in grace. As a result, Pilgrim's Progress became one of the most widely read books in English history, second only to the Bible in some eras, demonstrating how folk simplicity can be refined into high cultural profundity to edify believers and inspire moral conviction. C.S. Lewis, in his essay "On Stories" (1966), praised such works for their ability to convey "the huge, cosmic significance" through humble, folk-like forms, aligning with his own Narnia series, which cloaks Christian allegory in fairy-tale folklore while engaging high philosophical themes of sacrifice and resurrection.

Medieval Christian traditions further highlight this interdependence through mystery plays and liturgical dramas, such as the York Mystery Plays (14th–16th centuries) performed by English guilds. These were folk expressions at heart, community-driven theatrical retellings of biblical stories, from Creation to the Last Judgment, enacted in vernacular language on wagons in town squares for illiterate audiences. They incorporated local humor, songs, and customs, grounding sacred narratives in the people's daily lives. Yet, they aspired to high culture by drawing on scriptural exegesis and patristic theology, elevating simple performances into profound meditations on sin, salvation, and divine providence. Influenced by thinkers like Thomas Aquinas, who in Summa Theologica argued for the use of sensible images to convey spiritual truths, these plays bridged the folk's communal participation with the church's doctrinal depth, fostering widespread piety and cultural unity. Modern echoes can be seen in Passion plays like the Oberammergau Passion Play (performed since 1634 in Bavaria), which maintains folk traditions of village involvement while preserving a high degree of theological fidelity to the Gospels.

Even in hymnody, the symbiosis shines through. Many beloved Christian hymns, such as "Amazing Grace" (1779) by John Newton, originated from folk melodies and personal testimonies. Newton's raw account of his slave-trading past and conversion mirrors the confessional style of folk ballads. Yet, it was refined into high cultural expression through poetic structure and theological precision, emphasizing themes of unmerited grace drawn from Ephesians 2:8-9. Similarly, Charles Wesley's hymns, like "Hark! The Herald Angels Sing" (1739), blended folk carol traditions with sophisticated doctrinal content on the Incarnation, making them enduring staples in both rustic church gatherings and grand cathedral services. As Gene Edward Veith notes in The Spirituality of the Cross (1999), such hymns exemplify how Lutheran and broader Protestant traditions unite the folk's emotional immediacy with high confessional orthodoxy, countering the fragmentation of modern pop culture.

Mysticism and Humanism: Bridging Folk Devotion and High Theology

The synergy of folk and high culture, vital to countering materialism's shallow divide, finds profound expression in Christian mysticism and humanism, which unite earthy devotion with intellectual rigor to nurture souls rooted in God's truth. Johannes Tauler, a 14th-century Dominican mystic, preached in vernacular German, employing proverbs relatable to peasants and merchants to convey the soul's ascent to God. His sermons, influenced by Meister Eckhart, emphasize inner transformation through contemplative prayer, reflecting Bernard of Clairvaux's four degrees of love and ordering loves toward divine beauty. Tauler's pastoral exhortations grounded urban communities in shared faith while aspiring to transcendent union, fostering resilience against the distractions of his plague-ravaged era, much like the folk simplicity of Grimm's Fairy Tales elevated to moral insight.

Saint Anthony the Great, a 4th-century desert monk, embodied simplicity through his ascetic life, resisting demonic visions with spiritual discipline that inspired monasticism's high intellectual legacy. His story, recorded by Athanasius in *Life of Anthony*, blends relatable struggles akin to folk tales of heroic endurance with profound theology, fostering resilience against materialism's distractions. Augustine's mystical vision at Ostia (*Confessions*, 397), shared with his mother Monica, united folk-like emotional awe with philosophical insight into divine eternity, mirroring *Pilgrim's Progress*'s allegorical depth. This vision, a glimpse of God's beauty, counters the subjective "eye of the beholder" mantra rooting believers in objective truth.

Erasmus of Rotterdam, a 16th-century Christian humanist, bridged folk-friendly satire in The Praise of Folly (1511) with classical scholarship, editing Greek New Testament texts to reform education and foster virtuous elites. His work, like mystery plays, made theology accessible while aspiring to high moral ideals. These figures, Tauler's contemplative sermons, Anthony's desert faith, and Erasmus's scholarly reform, echo the Narnia chronicles, blending folk roots (fairy tales) with high theology (eucatastrophe). Classical education can revive their legacy, teaching students to meditate on Psalm 19:1 or study Tauler alongside Sir Gawain and the Green Knight in Socratic seminars, equipping academics to counter pop culture's shallowness and restore a culture where faith and reason harmonize, as C.S. Lewis's "Tao" urges (Chapter 2).

The Christian Imperative: Synergy Subordinated to the Gospel

While the synergy of folk and high cultures yields profound beauty and truth, as seen in the parables, *Pilgrim's Progress*, and mystery plays, this interplay must always submit to the corrections and authority of the Gospel. Scripture is the unchanging foundation around which all culture must be shaped, ensuring that human traditions, however enriching, do not eclipse divine revelation. Without this subordination, cultural expressions risk devolving into syncretism, where folk practices overlay and distort high theological truths, leading to a superficial faith that prioritizes ritual over redemption. As Deuteronomy 12:30-31 warns against adopting the detestable ways of surrounding nations, even under the guise of devotion, so too must Christian culture guard against blending that dilutes the Gospel's clarity: "Take care that you be not ensnared to follow them, after they have been destroyed before you, and that you do not inquire about their gods, saying, 'How did these nations serve their gods? that I also may do the same.' You shall not worship the Lord your God in that way, for every abominable thing that the Lord hates they have done for their gods" (ESV).

A clear example of what happens when cultural practices overshadow catechism is "Folk Catholicism" in the Philippines, a phenomenon born from Spanish colonial encounters with indigenous animism in the 16th century. Here, pre-Hispanic beliefs in spirits, ancestors, and nature, rooted in folk traditions, merged with Catholicism, creating a vibrant but often unorthodox piety. Devotees might venerate the Santo Niño (Child Jesus) with processions and fiestas yet incorporate anting-anting (amulets for protection) or rub handkerchiefs on sacred images to heal ailments, blending Christian symbols with pagan rituals for magical efficacy. While these practices foster communal identity and devotion, they often prioritize emotional fervor and superstitious acts over scriptural doctrines of salvation by faith (Ephesians 2:8-9), resulting in what scholars term "split-level Christianity," a surface adherence to Church teachings alongside deeper animist impulses.

The scholastic tradition, far from being an elitist luxury, is the indispensable guardian of objective beauty and truth against the acid of folk-subjectivism. The root error is the same: beauty and power are treated as subjective projections of the tribe rather than real participations in the transcendentals of Being itself. Thomas Aquinas, Richard Hooker, and the Lutheran orthodox alike insisted that goodness, truth, and beauty are the same reality as being itself—they inhere in things by divine act, not by cultural vote. When folk piety severs this ontological cord, waterfalls and sunsets, maternal love and communal fiestas, cease to be mirrors of the Triune Glory and become mere mirrors of collective feeling. The scholastic categories of substance, accident, analogy, and finality—precisely what Pusey and Vernon reclaimed for Anglican divinity—give every believer, high-born or low, the grammar to recognize that the beauty which stops a Manila street child in awe as she lights a candle before a simple wooden crucifix is the same objective splendor form that makes a rural Ilocano farmer fall silent when the rice terraces turn gold at dawn. Without this scholastic anchor, cultural renewal collapses into sentimental multiculturalism: "your beauty for your tribe, my beauty for mine." With it, the humblest folk hymn and the most soaring Tallis motet are revealed as finite echoes of the same uncreated Beauty, equally accessible to every human soul made in the image of God.

This overshadowing arose partly from historical factors: Spanish missionaries, outnumbered and variably trained, preached imperfect doctrines, allowing local folk elements to fill gaps and empower resistance to colonial subjugation. The result is a faith in which cultural rituals, such as ancestor-honoring in All Saints' Day observances or spirit-blessings on crops, can supplant catechetical formation, leading to a "paganism with Christianity as an addition" rather than a transformative submission to Christ. Such deviations must be avoided in Christian cultural renewal; folk traditions can enrich worship, as in the Simbang Gabi Christmas novenas that blend agrarian rhythms with Advent preparation, but only when rigorously tested against God's Word (Acts 17:11). Classical education, infused with Gospel fidelity, equips believers to discern and redeem these elements, ensuring synergy serves the Great Commission rather than cultural idolatry.

A Non-Christian Case Study: Japan's Cultural Fusion

While the focus of this book remains on Western Christian heritage, it is instructive to consider modern non-Christian examples that illustrate the enduring power of folk and high culture synergy in preserving societal values amid globalization. Japan, a highly successful society known for its conservative cultural ethos emphasizing harmony (*wa*), respect for tradition, and communal identity, offers a compelling case. Though not rooted in Christianity, Japan's media landscape demonstrates how a nation can maintain its historical roots while innovating in modern forms, blending indigenous folk elements with external influences, including historical German models from the Meiji era

(1868–1912) that shaped its modernization in law, medicine, and philosophy. This fusion has allowed Japan to resist some aspects of Western-style cultural downgrade more effectively than many societies, particularly in areas where the West has faltered: the deliberate preservation of folk traditions through government-backed initiatives and the elevation of everyday narratives into globally resonant high art.

This symbiosis is evident in Japan's jazz scene, where musicians like Nujabes (Seba Jun, 1974–2010) and his collaborator Uyama Hiroto integrated traditional Japanese aesthetics such as the serene minimalism of *wabi-sabi* (imperfect beauty drawn from folk pottery and tea ceremonies) with Western jazz and hip-hop, creating ethereal soundscapes that evoke introspection and harmony. Albums like Nujabes' *Metaphorical Music* (2003) or Uyama's *A Son of the Sun* (2008) draw from folk-like melodic simplicity and natural motifs (e.g., cherry blossoms symbolizing transience in haiku poetry), elevated through high-culture compositional complexity, resulting in music that honors classical beauty while appealing to contemporary audiences worldwide. In video games and anime, this dynamic thrives further: *Final Fantasy Tactics* (1997), a tactical RPG, weaves folk-inspired narratives of feudal warfare and chivalry, echoing Japan's samurai traditions from the *bushido* code, with profound high-culture explorations of ambition, betrayal, and societal decay, themes resonant with Machiavelli's *The Prince* in their cynical view of power and corruption. Similarly, the anime and visual novel *Steins; Gate* (2009–2011) employs sci-fi folk tropes of time travel and fate, refined into a high philosophical narrative grappling with regret, ethical paradoxes, and the moral costs of saving loved ones, blending emotional depth with intellectual rigor that invites viewers to ponder universal human frailty.

Japan's government initiatives, such as the Agency for Cultural Affairs' digital archives of manga, anime, and games, underscore a commitment to preserving these cultural assets as soft-power tools that export its values globally, even amid debates over content regulation for "wholesomeness" and moral uplift. This state-supported approach contrasts sharply with the West's education and corporate bailouts that prioritize profit over heritage, offering a model for how societies can institutionalize folk-high synergy to foster resilience. For instance, Studio Ghibli films like Hayao Miyazaki's *Spirited Away* (2001) masterfully fuse Shinto folk myths (spirits and yokai from oral tales) with high-art environmental and anti-war philosophy, achieving timeless appeal without the formulaic shallowness of many Hollywood blockbusters.

Yet, to avoid romanticizing Japan as an unblemished exemplar, we must acknowledge its own shadow issues that echo the materialistic "overdose" critiqued earlier and serve as a sobering reminder that no culture is immune without a transcendent foundation like Western Christian thought. Despite its achievements, Japan grapples with profound cultural erosion driven by corporate homogenization and demographic rootlessness. The anime and manga industries, dominated by conglomerates like Kadokawa Corporation and Bandai Namco, often commodify folk traditions for global export, diluting authentic narratives into sanitized, profit-driven tropes (e.g., the proliferation of "moe" character designs prioritizing cuteness over depth, or endless sequels in franchises like *One Piece* that stretch lore for merchandising). This mirrors where corporate algorithms and market demands erode philosophical nuance for broad appeal. Critics like cultural scholar Koichi Iwabuchi in *Recentering Globalization* (2002) argue that such "cultural hybridity" can lead to a loss of local specificity, turning sacred folk elements (e.g., kami spirits) into generic fantasy for international fans.

Moreover, Japan's hyper-modern society exacerbates isolation and spiritual emptiness, fostering a "rootless" generation vulnerable to the same distractions this book warns against. The rise of *hikikomori* (social recluses, estimated at over 1 million by government surveys in 2023) reflects how immersion in escapist pop culture, binge-watching anime or grinding video games can sever communal bonds, echoing Huxley's *Brave New World* pacification by entertainment. Demographic crises, including the world's lowest birth rate (1.26 in 2024 per UN data) and an aging population, signal a fraying of folk traditions like family festivals (*matsuri*) and intergenerational storytelling, as urban materialism prioritizes individual consumption over shared identity. Even government preservation efforts falter; debates over censorship. These challenges highlight that, without the moral anchor of Christian morality ordering loves toward the eternal societal successes, folk-high fusion remains fragile, susceptible to the corporate-government nexus that weaponizes culture for control.

This nuanced view of Japan thus enriches our argument: it celebrates achievements in areas the West has neglected, such as cultural archives that could inspire Christian homeschool networks or church-led media initiatives. Yet it underscores the dystopian risks of unmoored progressivism, urging a distinctly Christian renewal in which folk and high culture are not merely preserved but redeemed through Scripture's timeless truths. As G.K. Chesterton observed in Orthodoxy (1908), "Tradition is the democracy of the dead." It grants the departed a vote in the present, ensuring the living do not tyrannize the past with fleeting fashions; a principle Japan honors in form but, without the Incarnate Word, cannot fully animate with eternal life.

The Modern Divide and Corporate Exploitation

Today, however, a false dichotomy has emerged, perpetuated by a materialistic culture that devalues depth. Pop culture, when not weaponized, can bridge this divide, as seen in John Boorman's Excalibur (1981). Boorman drew on Arthurian folk legends, knights, quests, and the Grail's mythic pull while infusing Wagnerian grandeur and Malory's chivalric depth, forging a cinematic tapestry that grounded audiences in primal story yet elevated them toward transcendent ideals of sacrifice and destiny. Yet, corporate interests exploit the misconception that folk is "low" and high is "elitist," producing shallow content that neither grounds nor elevates. This corporate-driven divide reflects a broader cultural downgrade. By sidelining the humanities once central to classical education, society has lost the tools to appreciate the synergy of folk and high culture.

Reviving the Synergy Through Classical Education

By reviving classical education, as advocated by thinkers like those in A Handbook of Classical Lutheran Education, we can restore this symbiotic relationship, fostering a culture that values both the grounding tales of the folk and the aspirational heights of scholarly art. This renewal, rooted in Western Christian thought from Jesus' parables to Bunyan's allegories, equips us to resist the shallow tide of materialism and reclaim a heritage where depth and meaning prevail, as we will explore in the threats posed by corporate and government interests next.

Chapter 5: The Threat of Corporate/Government Interests

The symbiotic relationship between folk and high culture, nurtured by classical education, has historically served as a bulwark against societal decay, fostering communities grounded in shared heritage and elevated by intellectual rigor. Yet, this foundation faces an unprecedented assault from intertwined corporate and government interests that prioritize profit, control, and compliance over cultural depth and individual empowerment. Corporations, wielding vast financial and technological resources, homogenize culture into profit-driven commodities, while governments enable this erosion, undermining accountability and fostering corruption. This alliance not only dilutes our cultural heritage but also demoralizes society, leaving us vulnerable to manipulation and disconnected from the moral and intellectual tools needed to resist. The scandals involving figures like Jeffrey Epstein expose the moral rot at the core of this system, signaling a dystopian trajectory in which rootlessness and exploitation prevail unless countered by a revival of principled education and cultural renewal.

Corporate Homogenization: Commodifying Culture for Profit

Corporate dominance often reshapes cultural narratives for broad marketability, as seen in The Matrix sequels, where philosophical depth yielded to CGI spectacle prioritizing shareholder returns. This may not “always” be inherently malicious, but a symptom of unchecked profit motives, eroding authenticity." Megacorporations, driven by shareholder demands, exploit their control over intellectual properties to produce content that prioritizes broad marketability over the nuanced interplay of folk and high culture. Consider *The Matrix* (1999), a cultural milestone that blended folk-inspired cyberpunk myths, hackers and rebels rising against a dystopian system with high-culture philosophical inquiries into reality, free will, and human agency, drawing from Plato's cave allegory and Christian themes of awakening (John 8:32: "You will know the truth, and the truth will set you free"). The original film's mythic resonance, born from the Wachowskis' uncompromising vision, captivated audiences with its gritty folk roots (an everyman hero in Neo) and elevated reflections on existence. Yet, its sequels (*Reloaded* and *Revolutions*, 2003; *Resurrections*, 2021) succumbed to corporate pressures, bloating the narrative with convoluted subplots and CGI spectacle that overshadowed the original's soulful depth. Fan reactions lament the later films as "overproduced tangles," accusing studios of sanding down a profound story into a franchise churned for merchandising and box-office returns.

Similarly, The Witcher, rooted in Andrzej Sapkowski's books (1993–1999), exemplifies how corporations can erode cultural treasures. The novels weave Slavic folk tales, monsters, peasants, and gritty moral dilemmas reminiscent of the Nibelungenlied's raw heroism with high-culture explorations of power, betrayal, and ethical ambiguity, echoing Christian struggles with sin and redemption. Sapkowski's Geralt of Rivia, a monster hunter bound by principle, reflects the folk hero's grit and the high ideal of steadfast virtue, as seen in his maxim: "Evil is evil… but only the best have the courage to stick to their principles." The Netflix adaptation (2019–present), however, flattens this complexity for mass appeal, inserting modern political themes and streamlining the lore to fit bingeable episodes, often at the expense of the books' philosophical weight. Fans criticize the series for "sacrificing Sapkowski's nuance for algorithm-friendly drama," reflecting a corporate strategy that prioritizes global accessibility over the authentic interplay of folk grounding and high aspiration. This commodification sidelines independent creators and principled storytellers who honor authenticity, replacing their work with homogenized content tailored to the lowest common denominator.

This commodification is amplified by algorithmic manipulation, a hallmark of modern corporate strategy. Platforms like Netflix, YouTube, and TikTok use sophisticated algorithms to curate content that maximizes user engagement, often promoting shallow, emotionally manipulative productions over substantive works. These algorithms exploit psychological vulnerabilities, encouraging binge consumption through dopamine-driven feedback loops rather than fostering reflection or cultural enrichment. For example, Netflix's algorithm-driven originals, such as *The Kissing Booth* series (2018–2021), prioritize predictable romance and instant gratification over the layered narratives of classics like *The Pilgrim's Progress* or *The Divine Comedy*, which invite repeated exploration. This approach not only diminishes cultural depth but also marginalizes creators who resist corporate formulas, as algorithms favor content that aligns with profit-driven metrics over artistic merit.

Seneca and the Stoic Witness Against Imperial Corruption

Among the pagans the Church has most profitably plundered stands Seneca, the Roman Stoic who lived at the poisoned heart of empire yet never ceased to name its vices. Tutor and advisor to Nero, he saw wealth's tyranny, anger's madness, and the brevity of life squandered on luxury and power. In letters to Lucilius and essays *On Providence*, *On Anger*, and *On the Shortness of Life*, he taught detachment from fortune, mastery of passion, and the pursuit of virtue even when the palace walls dripped with corruption.

Though he knew not Christ, Seneca glimpsed truths the Gospel would later fulfill: that the soul can remain free though the body be enslaved, that adversity is training rather than punishment, and that no amount of gold can purchase a quiet conscience. Early Christians noted the resonance. Tertullian called him "often one of us"; Jerome listed him among the righteous; Augustine drank from the Stoic stream mediated through Cicero. Aquinas, harmonizing Aristotle with revelation, found in Stoic ethics a natural foundation for the cardinal virtues.

In our own age of corporate courtiers and government-sponsored decadence, where bailouts preserve the reckless while small craftsmen perish, where therapeutic codes silence dissent and elite networks evade justice, Seneca stands as a stern reminder that proximity to power need not mean complicity in its sins. His life was no martyrdom like Polycarp's, yet he dared critique the emperor's court from within it, and paid the price. When our young people study his letters alongside Paul's epistles or Bonhoeffer's prison writings, they learn that true eloquence speaks truth to tyrants, that virtue is not negotiable, and that the wise man prepares daily for the day when fidelity may cost everything.

Let the nominalist age call virtue quaint and the crony age call it impractical; we know better. Plunder Seneca gladly, baptize his hard-won wisdom, and send forth believers who, like him, refuse to let the palace corrupt the soul—even as they labor to reform the palace itself. For we have what Seneca lacked: the grace that transforms the will, the Cross that redeems suffering, and the hope of resurrection that turns every loss into gain.

Government Complicity: Undermining Education and Accountability

Government policies exacerbate this cultural downgrade, which prioritizes compliance and utility over critical thinking and cultural literacy. This model was designed to produce obedient citizens for industrial and military needs, as advocated by Johann Fichte's vision of state-controlled education. Its legacy persists in modern public schooling, where standardized curricula and testing regimes such as those mandated by the No Child Left Behind Act (2001) and Common Core Standards (2010), emphasize measurable outcomes over the humanities. This shift has systematically stripped education of its classical roots, disconnecting students from the folk and high cultural heritage that once fostered discernment and moral conviction.

A stark manifestation of this downgrade is the removal of classical literature from school curricula. In states like Florida, over 700 books, including literary classics like Margaret Atwood's *The Handmaid's Tale* and Richard Wright's *Native Son*, were banned or discontinued from K-12 schools in the 2023–2024 academic year, often under the guise of avoiding "controversial" content. Similarly, works like *To Kill a Mockingbird* and *The Great Gatsby* have been removed in various districts for perceived sensitivities, replaced with young adult novels that prioritize accessibility over depth. These bans, while sometimes framed as protecting students, erode their exposure to complex narratives that challenge moral and intellectual growth, leaving them less equipped to engage with their cultural heritage or question authority. The decline of cursive writing instruction, removed from Common Core in 2010, further isolates students from historical documents like the U.S. Constitution or personal letters from figures like Thomas Jefferson, hindering their ability to connect with primary sources. While states like California have begun reinstating cursive due to public outcry, its absence for over a decade has already widened the gap between generations and their historical roots.

Civic rituals that once reinforced shared identity have also been eroded. The national anthem, though not banned outright, has faced declining emphasis in schools due to controversies over its performance, rooted in protests and legal precedents like *West Virginia State Board of Education v. Barnette* (1943), which protects students' rights to abstain from patriotic exercises. This has led many districts to reduce or eliminate anthem-related routines, diminishing opportunities for communal bonding through folk traditions. These educational shifts, justified by "practicality" or "inclusivity," align with the Prussian model's focus on producing compliant workers rather than critical thinkers, creating a populace more susceptible to corporate-driven pop culture and less capable of resisting systemic corruption.

Economic policies further entrench this corporate-government nexus. The 2008 financial crisis exposed stark double standards, as the U.S. government's Troubled Asset Relief Program (TARP) funneled $700 billion to bail out banks like Citigroup and AIG, preserving corporate giants despite their reckless practices. Meanwhile, millions of small businesses, often rooted in local communities and principled craftsmanship, collapsed without equivalent support, leading to widespread foreclosures and job losses. This favoritism undermines the free market's natural corrective mechanism, in which failing corporations should give way to innovative, smaller entities. Instead, bailouts perpetuate a system where corporate elites thrive on unaccountability, demoralizing citizens who see their principles and livelihoods devalued. The 2020 COVID-19 bailouts repeated this pattern, with large corporations receiving billions while small businesses struggled to access relief, further eroding trust in governance.

Government surveillance and data-sharing partnerships with corporations add another layer of control. Programs like PRISM, exposed by Edward Snowden in 2013, revealed how agencies like the NSA collaborate with tech giants Google, Apple, and Microsoft to collect user data, often under the pretext of national security. This erodes personal autonomy as citizens are conditioned to accept oversight without questioning its cultural or moral implications. Such policies divert attention from corporate homogenization, creating a feedback loop where a less-educated populace, stripped of cultural roots, is more easily manipulated by both state and corporate agendas.

Christian Perspectives: Resisting the Tyranny of Materialism

In the quiet annals of those who ponder the soul's hidden fractures, one might discern in this corporate-government weave a shadow of ancient idolatry, not the golden calves of old, but the subtler gleam of mammon, where the clamor of wealth and dominion eclipses the still voice of the divine. As our Lord observed in Matthew 6:24, with that piercing clarity that unmasks our divided hearts, “No one can serve two masters... You cannot serve God and money.” Here, in the love of riches and sway that animates corporate ventures and governmental pacts alike, we glimpse a disordering of affections that harmonious ascent where love ascends first to God, and all else falls into rightful place. Such a misalignment, like a garden overgrown with thorns, permits the quiet flourishing of shadows in high places; consider the 1MDB scandal, where over $4.5 billion was looted from Malaysia's sovereign wealth fund between 2009 and 2015, funneled through global banks like Goldman Sachs to finance Hollywood films like The Wolf of Wall Street and lavish elite indulgences, as revealed in 2025's ongoing trials and asset seizures. This web of greed, shielded by corporate profits and lax oversight, distracts society with glittering pop culture spectacles, allowing hidden injustices to linger like unpruned weeds in the soul's quiet corners.

Christian thinkers offer a robust critique of this threat. Francis Schaeffer, in *How Should We Then Live?* (1976) argues that the shift from biblical foundations to humanistic autonomy has enabled corporate and government manipulation, replacing transcendent truth with relativistic values that serve elite interests. Os Guinness, in *Renaissance: The Power of the Gospel However Dark the Times* (2014), calls for Christians to resist this by publicly engaging culture, countering the privatization of faith that allows materialism to dominate.

The Book of Romans provides further insight, describing cultural decline as a consequence of exchanging God's glory for created things: "For although they knew God, they did not honor him as God or give thanks to him, but they became futile in their thinking, and their foolish hearts were darkened" (Romans 1:21). This passage mirrors the modern replacement of folk and high culture with corporate-driven ephemera, leaving society vulnerable to manipulation. John MacArthur, in his sermon "Overcoming Materialism" (1980), emphasizes that true joy comes from prioritizing heavenly treasures, urging believers to detach from the transient allure of corporate content and government-sanctioned conformity.

Distributist Warnings: Chesterton and Coulombe on the Corporate-Government Leviathan

Amid this modern convergence of corporate profit and governmental coercion, the prescient voices of G.K. Chesterton and Charles A. Coulombe rise as prophetic sentinels, diagnosing the alliance not as mere economic inefficiency but as a spiritual and societal monstrosity, a "Servile State" that devours the small, the local, and the free. Chesterton, the architect of distributism, beheld in the early 20th century the ominous fusion of "Hudge" (big government) and "Gudge" (big business), two pretended antagonists who in truth conspire to displace the independent yeoman, the family farm, and the guild craftsman with a proletarian horde dependent on wages, subsidies, and bureaucratic edicts. "Big Business and State Socialism are very much alike," he quipped in *The Outline of Sanity* (1926), "especially Big Business." This partnership, he argued, does not liberate but enslaves, homogenizing culture into factory output while eroding the folk-high interplay that once animated authentic human communities. The result is a cultural desert where the living memory of folk wisdom passed through generations in proverbs, ballads, and craft is replaced by algorithmically curated ephemera, and high ideals are subordinated to quarterly earnings reports.

Chesterton's parable of Hudge and Gudge in *What's Wrong with the World* (1910) remains eerily prescient: the state promises welfare, the corporation efficiency, yet both deliver tenements, chain stores, and a populace stripped of property and purpose. This is no accident but the inevitable fruit of concentrated power. Government shields monopolies through tariffs, patents, and regulations that crush small competitors. Consider the 2023 U.S. antitrust case against Amazon, where the FTC documented how the company used predatory pricing and third-party data to eliminate independent booksellers, driving 40 % of local bookstores out of business since 2010 (American Booksellers Association). Meanwhile, corporations fund the expansion of state control through lobbying: OpenSecrets data for 2024 shows the U.S. Chamber of Commerce alone spent $94 million to influence legislation favoring corporate tax breaks and deregulation. The result? A commodified culture echoing the algorithmic flattening of *The Matrix* sequels or *The Witcher* adaptations, where folk myths are sanitized for global markets, and high ideals are subordinated to shareholder value. As Chesterton warned in *The Superstition of Divorce* (1920), "The family is the test of freedom," and when both Hudge and Gudge conspire to dissolve it through wage dependency, urban uprooting, and cultural amnesia, freedom itself becomes a relic.

Chesterton's antidote was radical in its simplicity: **distributism**, a "third way" that breaks up concentrations of wealth via laws favoring widespread ownership guilds, cooperatives, family enterprises rooted in Catholic subsidiarity and the dignity of the person over the machine. He envisioned a society where the baker owns his oven, the farmer his land, and the storyteller his voice, not as romantic nostalgia, but as a practical bulwark against servility. "Three acres and a cow," his famous slogan, was not a pastoral fantasy but an economic program: redistribute idle land via taxation on unearned increments (as proposed in *The Outline of Sanity*), protect small shops through anti-chain-store legislation, and revive guilds to regulate quality and wages without state socialism. In cultural terms, this meant preserving the folk vitality of local festivals (e.g., the English village fair) and high craftsmanship (e.g., illuminated manuscripts) against mass-produced kitsch. Chesterton saw clearly that without property, there is no stake in culture; without culture, no resistance to manipulation.

Soft on Predators, Ruthless on the Harmless: The Inversion of Justice

The same government that bails out reckless banks with $700 billion (TARP, 2008) and surveils citizens via PRISM shows a bizarre inversion of justice in its criminal code. Murderers and rapists—crimes that shatter the imago Dei and destroy folk communities—routinely receive sentences of 10 years or less, often with early parole. In 2024, the average sentence for murder in the U.S. was ~16 years (Bureau of Justice Statistics), with many serving under 10 due to plea deals. Rape? ~7–9 years on average, with 40% of convicted rapists serving 5 or fewer (DOJ, 2023).

Meanwhile, victimless crimes—drug possession, tax evasion, or even speech crimes (e.g., "hate speech" violations in Europe)—are met with disproportionate resources and sentences. The U.S. spends $80 billion annually on the War on Drugs (Drug Policy Alliance, 2025), imprisoning ~500,000 for non-violent offenses, while only 1 in 6 rapists will ever spend a day in jail (RAINN, 2025). In the UK, Operation Soteria (2024–2025) poured £100 million into policing online speech, while 93% of reported rapes went unprosecuted (Home Office, 2025).

This is not justice—it is therapeutic tyranny masquerading as compassion. The state protects the predator (often elite, as in Epstein's plea deal) while criminalizing the common man. The folk wisdom of "an eye for an eye" and the high ideal of lex talionis (rooted in Exodus 21:24) are abandoned for a system that fears offending the violent but crushes the harmless. This is the Servile State in action: control through selective enforcement, where the yeoman is policed into submission, but the wolf walks free.

Charles A. Coulombe: Reviving the Corporate State as Antidote

Charles A. Coulombe, a contemporary torchbearer of Chesterton's vision, sharpens this critique while charting a structured path forward through **Catholic corporatism**. In works like *Quest for the Catholic State* (2018) and *A Catholic Quest for the Holy Grail* (2017), he condemns the liberal order's destruction of medieval guilds, the "old corporations" which once harmonized labor and capital under Christian ethics, giving way to industrial squalor, socialist backlash, and oligarchic rule. Modern crony capitalism, he argues, is the poisoned fruit: a corporate-government nexus that bailouts preserve (as in 2008's TARP or 2020's CARES Act, where $500 billion went to large corporations while 22 million small business jobs vanished, U.S. Census Bureau, 2021), surveils through PRISM-like pacts with Google and Microsoft, and culturally lobotomizes via algorithmic dopamine. Netflix's 2023 decision to crack down on password-sharing, for instance, was not just a revenue grab but a symbolic assertion of control over the domestic sphere, turning the family living room into a metered utility.

Yet Coulombe refuses despair. He revives the **Corporate State** as envisioned by Popes Leo XIII (*Rerum Novarum*, 1891) and Pius XI (*Quadragesimo Anno*, 1931): not the fascist caricature of Mussolini's *Carta del Lavoro* (1927), which subordinated guilds to the state, but a society organized into **professional corporations** modern guilds encompassing workers, owners, and professionals in each industry, overseen by the state only to enforce justice, fair wages, and quality without class warfare or monopoly. These bodies would be voluntary, rooted in subsidiarity, and animated by natural law and sacramental vision. A baker's corporation, for example, would include master bakers, journeymen, apprentices, and suppliers setting standards for bread quality, training the young in both craft and ethics, and resolving disputes internally before any state intervention. This is not central planning but **ordered liberty**: the state as referee, not owner.

Coulombe's model directly counters cultural homogenization. Guilds would foster **artisanal media** independent podcast networks, local publishing houses, and folk music collectives free from Silicon Valley gatekeeping. Imagine a "Storytellers' Corporation" certifying oral historians, funding regional myth revivals (e.g., Appalachian jack tales or Cajun *contes*), and producing audio dramas that blend folk cadence with theological depth, distributed via decentralized platforms like Substack or Mastodon, not Spotify's 70 % market chokehold (MIDiA Research, 2024). High culture thrives too: a "Scholars' Corporation" could accredit classical academies, ensuring Latin, logic, and Scripture are taught with rigor, while collaborating with folk corporations to stage mystery plays or Shakespeare in vernacular settings.

The Economic Machinery of the Servile State: Tariffs, Taxes, and the Death of Localism

If Chesterton diagnosed the disease and Coulombe prescribed the guild, then the tax-trade complex is the pathogen, and protectionist distributism is the vaccine.

The Servile State does not arise by accident. It is engineered, line by line, in the U.S. Code, the WTO schedule, and the lobbyist's retainer. Two legislative acts—the Sixteenth Amendment (1913) and the reciprocal lowering of tariffs (1945–2001)—function as the twin pistons of a machine that extracts wealth from the locality, concentrates it in the metropolis, and returns it only as debt, regulation, and cultural homogenization. The result is not merely economic inefficiency; it is spiritual dispossession—the slow strangulation of the independent yeoman, the family firm, and the parish economy that once sustained both folk vitality and high aspiration.

I. The Fiscal Extraction Engine: From Tariff to Income Tax

Era	Primary Federal Revenue	Avg. Tariff Rate	Top Marginal Income-Tax Rate
1790–1913	**Tariffs (90–95 %)**	**20–50 %**	**0 %**
1913–1945	Transition	**15–30 %**	**7–77 %**
1945–2000	**Income & Payroll (70 %)**	**5–15 %**	**35–91 %**
2001–2025	**Income & Payroll (80 %)**	**~1.5 %**	**37 %**

Sources: U.S. Treasury, IRS SOI, WTO Tariff Database.

The **Sixteenth Amendment** severed the federal government from the customs house. Where once the port collector in Charleston or Boston remitted duties that were immediately recycled into local canals, courthouses, and militias, the income tax created a vertical siphon: wages earned in Peoria are garnished in Washington, D.C., and returned—if at all—as means-tested grants that come laced with federal strings. The tariff, meanwhile, was transformed from a revenue backbone to a negotiating chip in the great game of global trade.

The consequence is stark. In 1890 the McKinley Tariff raised the effective rate on dutiable imports to 48 %; within a decade American industrial wages rose 50 % (Irwin, NBER 1998). In 2023 the average applied tariff on Chinese goods is 3.1 %; manufacturing employment has fallen from 19.6 million (1979) to 13.0 million (2024), with the steepest losses in counties that once produced textiles, steel, and furniture—the very folk industries that anchored Main Street.

II. The Trade-Offshoring Flywheel

The mechanism is mathematical and merciless:

1. **Tariff = 0 % → Landed cost gap** between U.S. labor ($25/hr + benefits) and Vietnamese labor ($3/hr) = **$22/hr**.

2. **Corporate tax code** permits **indefinite deferral** of foreign profits → **Apple parks $252 billion offshore** (2017–2023).

3. **Stock buybacks** (legalized 1982) → **$1.2 trillion repatriated under TCJA 2017 → 95 % used for buybacks/dividends**, not new U.S. plant (Lazonick, 2023).

4. **Lobbying → $4.1 billion in 2024** (OpenSecrets) → **MFN status for China (2000)** passes **83–15** in Senate.

The local firm cannot compete. A regional textile mill in Gastonia, North Carolina, pays full freight on payroll taxes,

OSHA compliance, and environmental permits. Walmart imports the same fabric from Bangladesh, deducts the import as a cost of goods sold, and writes off the distribution center under bonus depreciation. The mill closes; the county's property-tax base shrinks by 18 % in five years; the school levy fails; the children leave.

Quantitative impact: The China Shock (1999–2011) eliminated 2.4 million U.S. jobs, with 75 % of losses in counties below the 25th percentile of median income (Autor, Dorn, Hanson, 2021). Every $1,000 of imported goods displaced $1,400 in local wages—a net loss of $400 that never recirculates.

III. The Cultural Collateral Damage

The buffet is the perfect microcosm. In 1985, Old Country Buffet opened in Dubuque, Iowa: patrons pay at the door, serve themselves, and trust prevails. By 2008, the chain filed Chapter 11; by 2023, 80 % of locations were shuttered. The stated reasons—rising food costs, labor shortages—are symptoms. The root cause is shrinkage: patrons overloading plates, smuggling food, or simply walking out. High-trust Japan runs conveyor-belt sushi with cameras and RFID plates; the U.S. equivalent fails because no one knows their neighbor.

The **economic numbers** tell the same story:

Metric	**1970**	**2024**
% retail spending at **independent stores**	**65 %**	**28 %**
% grocery dollars at **local chains**	**70 %**	**15 %**

Metric	**1970**	**2024**
Independent pharmacies	**55,000**	**19,000**
Community bank assets	**40 %**	**13 %**

Source: USDA, FDIC, IBISWorld.

A dollar spent locally circulates 3–7 times longer than one spent at a chain (American Independent Business Alliance). When the local hardware store closes, the Little League loses its sponsor; when the regional grocer shutters, the church food pantry loses its discount. The folk culture—the Friday fish fry, the county fair, the parish picnic—starves.

IV. The Distributist-Corporatist Antidote: A Policy Trinity

Chesterton's three acres and a cow and Coulombe's professional corporations are not nostalgic; they are prescriptive. The economic machinery can be reversed with three interlocking reforms:

1. **Tariff Revenue Ring-Fenced to Place**
    - **10–20 % baseline tariff** on non-allied imports.
    - **100 % of revenue** allocated to **states by import volume** (e.g., California ports → California schools).
    - **Projected yield**: **$200–250 billion/year** (CBO 2025).
2. **Tax Small, Punish Scale**

  - **0 % federal income tax** on firms **<500 employees.**
  - **Progressive surcharge** on firms **>10,000 employees** (1 % per 5,000 above threshold).
  - **Eliminate bonus depreciation** for **offshore-parented entities.**

3. **No Buybacks for Tariff Beneficiaries**
  - Any firm receiving **>5 % of revenue from tariff-protected markets → 100 % reinvestment mandate** in U.S. plant, training, or R&D.
  - **Violations: clawback of tariff savings + 10 % penalty.**

Historical precedent:

- **South Korea (1962–1987)**: **50 % tariffs + zero income tax on SMEs →** GDP per capita **$80 → $12,000.**
- **Germany (post-2008)**: **Buyback ban + apprenticeship levy → Mittelstand = 60 % of employment.**

V. The Theological Warrant

The Servile State is not merely inefficient; it is idolatrous. It replaces the vocational order—where the baker owns his oven, the farmer his land, and the storyteller his voice—with the mammonic order, where profit is god, scale is sacrament, and localism is sin.

"No one can serve two masters… You cannot serve God and money." (Matthew 6:24)

The tariff is not a regressive tax; it is a tithe on the importer, a liturgical act that re-embeds exchange in place. The local tax break is not a subsidy; it is justice, restoring the widow's mite to the parish rather than the hedge fund.

When the shrimp is caught in Louisiana, the tax stays in Baton Rouge, and the lobbyist cannot afford a G650, the buffet reopens—and the stranger at the table is recognized as neighbor.

Historical Catholic Corporatist Models: Lessons in Resistance

Coulombe points to three 20th-century experiments, flawed, brief, and crushed by liberal-capitalist victors of WWII, as proof of concept. Each resisted the corporate-government leviathan by restructuring economy and culture around vocation, faith, and localism.

Coulombe's Exemplars	Key Anti-Servile Features
Portugal under Salazar (Estado Novo, 1933–1968)	Industry-specific corporations ended strikes; state-mediated labor-capital harmony; protected small farms and faith-based culture.
Austria under Dollfuss (1933–1934)	Corporative constitution replaced parliament; economic councils elevated Church social teaching; resisted Nazi/corporate encroachment.
Spain's Falange Syndicates (post-1939)	Vertical syndicates by sector ensured mutual duties; curbed foreign capital; fostered folk traditions amid high civic aspiration.

These regimes were authoritarian in governance. Salazar jailed dissidents, Franco executed Republicans, but their economic and cultural structures were subsidiarist, not totalitarian. They prove that binding business and government under ethical oversight can resist servility. Unlike Chesterton's broadside against all centralization, Coulombe wields a purified partnership as the sword against the threat: corporations tamed by guild self-regulation, government restrained by natural law and papal social teaching, culture revived through vocational bodies that honor folk craftsmanship (e.g., a Brewers' Corporation ensuring monastic ale recipes survive) alongside high intellectual pursuit (e.g., a Philosophers' Corporation debating Aquinas in public squares).

Together, Chesterton and Coulombe unveil the corporate-government alliance as a counterfeit trinity profit, power, propaganda usurping God's order. Their distributist-corporatist vision aligns seamlessly with classical education's mission: to form souls who own their tools, question their masters, and weave folk vitality with eternal truth. In an age where Epstein's scandals reveal elite rot shielded by this nexus, their call is urgent: dismantle the leviathan through property, vocation, and virtue, lest the Servile State become our eternal matrix.

A Personal Postscript: Ecumenical Distributism and Ordered Liberty

As an Anglican standing in the via media of Scripture, reason, and tradition, I must confess a personal caveat to this distributist-corporatist vision, one that widens the tent rather than narrowing it to a Roman enclosure. While Coulombe's retrieval of the Corporate State stirs the imagination, my own path would be resolutely **ecumenical**, inviting Orthodox, Reformed, Lutheran, and even Baptist brethren to the guildhall table. The Book of Common Prayer's liturgy, Hooker's laws of ecclesiastical polity, and the Thirty-Nine Articles' balance of faith and freedom offer a supple framework: guilds and cooperatives animated by the Gospel, not the Code of Canon Law; subsidiarity rooted in the parish and the shire, not the curia. Let the baker be Anglican, the brewer Presbyterian, the storyteller Pentecostal, so long as each owns his oven, honors the Sabbath, and crafts with excellence unto the Lord.

I am cautious of authoritarianism. A staunch defender of the Second Amendment, I believe the yeoman's rifle and the farmer's plow are twin guardians of liberty; "innocent until proven guilty" is not mere jurisprudence but a reflex of Imago Dei justice. Yet I am equally convinced that public society must be deliberately ordered toward virtue. Degeneracy, whether the algorithmic pornography of OnlyFans or the state-sanctioned mutilation of children in the name of "gender care," has no claim to the commons. The public square is not neutral; it is a garden that must be weeded. Thus, I would boldly assert: **no one should hold public office who does not openly profess the Creeds and live under the discipline of a Christian congregation.** Not as a theocratic bludgeon, but as a minimal covenant: if the magistrate will not bow the knee to Christ, how shall he rule in His stead? This is no innovation; it is the spirit of Alfred the Great's Doom Book, of the colonial charters that required oaths upon the Gospels, of the Anglican divines who framed limited government within a Christian cosmos.

Here, then, is my personal distributist wager: widespread property, vocational guilds, and ecumenical confession as the threefold cord against the Servile State. Not top-down fiat, but bottom-up covenant, parish guilds funding classical academies, county assemblies chartering artisan cooperatives, a national council of churches accrediting magistrates who fear God more than polls. The muskets remain in the homes of freeholders; the ballots are cast by disciples; the culture is sung in hymns and forged in forges. This is no utopia, but a return to the shire-moot and the cathedral close where folk vitality and high aspiration meet under the cross, and the corporate-government leviathan is slain, not by the sword of the state, but by the quiet revolution of three acres, a cow, and a child who prays the Magnificat at twilight.

Historical Parallels: Lessons from Past Resistance

Historically, societies that resisted cultural and moral decay relied on educated citizens grounded in their heritage. The American Founding Fathers, despite their classical liberal leanings, recognized education's role in preventing tyranny. John Jay, devout Christian and first Chief Justice of the Supreme Court, declared, "I consider knowledge to be the soul of a republic… and that the diffusion of it among the people is to be the principal means of preserving their liberties." John Adams echoed this, stating, "Liberty cannot be preserved without a general knowledge among the people, who have a right... to knowledge." Their vision, rooted in classical education principles informed by Christian virtue, fostered a generation capable of drafting documents like the Declaration of Independence, which drew on folk traditions of communal rights and high philosophical ideals from Locke and Montesquieu.

The Protestant Reformation offers another parallel. Martin Luther, in his 1524 treatise, argued that education in Scripture and classical languages was essential to counter ecclesiastical corruption and societal decay. By equipping believers to read the Bible and engage with cultural heritage, Luther empowered a movement that challenged the Catholic Church's monopoly on truth, fostering a culture of accountability and reform. This historical precedent underscores the power of education to resist centralized control, whether from medieval clergy or modern corporate-government alliances.

The Path Forward: Education as Resistance

The corporate-government threat to cultural depth demands a return to classical education, which unites folk and high culture to foster critical thinkers and principled citizens. Initiatives like the Association of Classical Christian Schools (ACCS) and the Consortium for Classical and Lutheran Education demonstrate this potential, reviving the Trivium and Great Books curricula to produce students who excel in critical thinking and cultural engagement. These programs counter by prioritizing depth over compliance, equipping students to discern truth amid corporate noise and government overreach.

The Anglican tradition, with its rich synthesis of Scripture, reason, and tradition, offers a compelling framework for this educational revival. In "Fare Forward": The Influence of Christian Humanism on the Classical Christian Education Movement, Bradford Littlejohn argues that Christian humanism, rooted in the Anglican commitment to a faith-informed intellect, equips students to engage culture with discernment and moral clarity. By grounding education in the liturgical rhythms of the Book of Common Prayer and the classical pursuit of truth, beauty, and goodness, Anglicanism provides a robust antidote to the corporate-government alliance that commodifies culture and erodes accountability. This approach, as Littlejohn suggests, empowers communities to reclaim their heritage through schools that integrate folk traditions such as hymnody and local storytelling with high cultural aspirations, fostering citizens who can resist the shallow allure of materialism and demand a society rooted in transcendent values.

Christian communities can lead this resistance by fostering education that integrates Scripture with classical learning, as advocated by Gregory of Nazianzus and Martin Luther. By teaching students to engage with works like *The Pilgrim's Progress* which blends folk allegory with theological depth which unites mythic storytelling with philosophical rigor, churches and schools can cultivate a generation that values meaning over materialism. This revival extends beyond academics; it involves communities reclaiming folk traditions, local festivals, hymns, and stories while aspiring to high cultural excellence.

The consequences of inaction are dire. Without resistance, the corporate-government nexus will continue to erode cultural roots, producing a dystopian society where shallow pop culture and unaccountable elites dominate. Yet, by recognizing this threat and reviving classical education, we can empower individuals to reclaim their heritage, demand accountability, and build a culture rooted in truth, beauty, and virtue. As we explore in the chapters ahead, this path to renewal begins with small, principled acts within homes, churches, and schools that collectively restore our cultural soul.

Chapter 6: The Dystopian Consequences of Cultural Loss

The erosion of folk and high culture, driven by the decline of classical education and the rise of materialism, has left society unmoored, chasing fleeting pop culture trends while losing its grounding in community and aspiration. This cultural loss is not merely an aesthetic tragedy; it carries profound, dystopian consequences. A society disconnected from its roots, lacking the shared identity of folk culture and the intellectual elevation of high culture, becomes rootless, vulnerable to manipulation, and ripe for centralized control. This trajectory, marked by elite corruption and a populace ill-equipped to challenge it, mirrors the warnings of dystopian literature and threatens to transform our world into one where shallow distractions reign supreme, eroding moral conviction and communal bonds. Yet, by understanding these consequences through a deepened Christian lens, we can chart a path toward renewal through the revival of classical education and the reclamation of cultural depth rooted in Western Christian thought.

The Rootlessness of a Culture Adrift

The loss of folk and high culture creates a rootless society, one without the anchors of communal identity or transcendent ideals. Folk culture, with its oral traditions, local myths, and shared rituals, fosters a sense of belonging that binds communities across generations. High culture, through its philosophical and artistic achievements, challenges individuals to aspire to truth, beauty, and virtue. Together, they provide a balanced foundation: folk culture grounds us in the collective human experience, while high culture elevates us toward universal truths. Without these, society drifts, susceptible to the whims of corporate narratives and government agendas that thrive on a disconnected populace.

This rootlessness manifests globally in escalating culture wars, riots, and spiritual disconnection, fueled by a vanity-driven materialism where personal status trumps communal bonds. In 2025, protests and riots surged worldwide, with the Carnegie Endowment's 2025 Global Protest Tracker reporting over 80,000 incidents in 2024, projected to rise 10% in 2025, often tied to economic hardship and identity fragmentation. Examples include Indonesia's deadly demonstrations against economic slowdown and police brutality, drawing hundreds of thousands (Reuters, 2024), Iran's nationwide uprisings against regime corruption (Amnesty International, 2025), and Kenya's ongoing discontent, where 57% see no progress amid protests (Afrobarometer, 2025). These reflect a deeper vanity: Gen Z's focus on material displays, driven by social media influencers, where global material use has tripled since the 1970s, correlating with poorer well-being (UN Environment Programme, Global Resources Outlook 2024). This "endless renewal" of status-seeking imprisons individuals in shallow pursuits, echoing Ecclesiastes 1:2's warning: "Vanity of vanities! All is vanity."

Church attendance underscores this crisis: In the West, the Pew Research Center's 2025 Religious Trends Report projects 15,000 U.S. church closures in 2025, with attendance at 30% and many below pre-pandemic levels, while Europe sees similar trends amid secularism (European Values Study, 2024). Globally, however, Christianity grows at 1.27% annually, with Evangelical surges in Africa and Asia offering resilient models (World Christian Database, 2025). Yet, this rootlessness amplifies mental health woes: The World Health Organization's 2024 Global Health Estimates reports 5.7% of adults suffer from depression (over 280 million cases), with women more affected; in the U.S., the CDC's 2024 National Health Interview Survey finds 13.1% of adolescents and adults aged 12+ experienced depression. Gen Z faces heightened rates 46% diagnosed with mental health conditions, 42% battling depression and hopelessness linked to social media comparison (39%) and uncertain futures (American Psychological Association, 2025 Stress in America). This epidemic, equivalent to smoking 15 cigarettes daily in health risks, disrupts faith communities, as Hebrews 10:25 urges gathering together. Amid this, Gen Z shows a slow pivot toward traditionalism: The Pew Research Center's 2025 Youth Faith Survey finds Gen Z Christians rose to 51% (from 45% in 2023), with Catholic converts climbing and youth embracing family units, religion, and conservatism as rebellion against secular chaos, evident in voter data and X discussions on "Gen Z conservatism" (Gallup, 2025 Election Trends). From a Christian view, rejecting God's glory for vain idols leads to futile thinking.

Amid this, Gen Z shows a slow pivot toward traditionalism: In 2025, Gen Z Christians rose to 51% (from 45% in 2023), with Catholic converts climbing and youth embracing family units, religion, and conservatism as rebellion against secular chaos.

This disconnection breeds vulnerability to manipulation. George Orwell's 1984 (1949) warned of a dystopian world where simplified language ("Newspeak") and constant surveillance strip individuals of critical thinking, making them pliable to authoritarian control. Similarly, Aldous Huxley's Brave New World (1932) envisioned a society pacified by shallow entertainment and chemical distractions, a chilling parallel to today's algorithm-driven streaming platforms and social media feeds. Both novels underscore the danger of a populace trained to consume rather than question. The National Assessment of Educational Progress (NAEP) highlights this crisis: in 2024, 40% of fourth-graders scored below basic reading proficiency, a 5-point drop since 2019, reflecting a decline in the skills needed to engage with complex texts or challenge manipulative narratives. This educational failure leaves society ill-equipped to resist the homogenized content churned out by corporations like Disney or Netflix, which prioritize profit over substance.

To extend this, consider the epidemic of loneliness as a modern symptom of rootlessness, where digital interactions supplant genuine communal bonds. The U.S. Surgeon General's 2023 advisory on loneliness, reiterated in 2025 updates, warns that social isolation affects over half of U.S. adults, contributing to health risks equivalent to smoking 15 cigarettes a day. This crisis, amplified by platforms that promise connection but deliver superficial engagement, echoes Huxley's pacified society, where individuals are conditioned to avoid meaningful relationships. From a Christian vantage, this isolation erodes the communal essence of faith, as seen in Hebrews 10:25's exhortation not to forsake gathering together. Yet, as Surgeon General Vivek Murthy noted in 2025, antidotes lie in rebuilding intentional relationships, opportunities for churches to foster embodied communities that counter digital fragmentation.

Cultural Rot: The Justification of Violence in a Degraded Society

The rootlessness engendered by cultural loss extends beyond mere disconnection from heritage; it festers into a profound societal decay, manifesting in a chilling disregard for human life and the normalization of violence as a tool for ideological ends.

This rot is starkly evident in a series of violent acts that have scarred the nation, each revealing the depth of moral erosion in our polarized age. On July 13, 2024, former President Donald Trump narrowly survived an assassination attempt during a campaign rally in Butler, Pennsylvania, when a gunman, Thomas Matthew Crooks, fired eight shots from a rooftop, grazing Trump's ear, killing one attendee, and injuring two others. The tragedy, as reported by sources like NPR, was met with shocking responses on social media, where some celebrated the attack as "deserved" or lamented its failure, exposing a fractured society where empathy yields to enmity. Similarly, the assassination of Charlie Kirk, the influential conservative activist and founder of Turning Point USA, on September 10, 2025, during his "American Comeback" tour at Utah Valley University in Orem, Utah, marked another grim milestone. Kirk was fatally shot in the neck from a rooftop before a crowd of 3,000, leaving behind a wife and two young children. Fox News and BBC reported the aftermath, noting how online mobs cheered his death as "justice," amplifying fears among public figures. Further compounding this crisis, the June 2025 shootings of Democratic lawmakers in Minnesota saw House Speaker Emerita Melissa Hortman and her husband, Mark, murdered in their home, while State Senator John Hoffman and his wife, Yvette, survived a targeted attack. Described by the FBI as "horrific acts of targeted violence," these killings, reported by CNN and Al Jazeera, underscore the indiscriminate nature of this bloodshed, striking across political divides and intensifying a sense of vulnerability nationwide.

These events, the attempted assassination of Trump, the murder of Kirk, and the Minnesota shootings, are not isolated but symptoms of a cultural downgrade that has simmered for decades, where the sanctity of life is casually dismissed in the name of partisan fervor. From a Christian perspective, humanity exchanges "the truth about God for a lie," worshipping created ideologies over the Creator. The loss of folk culture's communal bonds, once fostering shared humanity through stories of redemption and kinship, and high culture's call to virtue, as seen in Athanasius's vision of the incarnate image or Bonhoeffer's costly grace, leaves society vulnerable to dehumanizing its opponents. Social media amplifies this, with algorithms fueling outrage cycles that reward vitriol, as seen in posts celebrating Kirk's death, rationalizing the attack on Trump as "retribution," or selectively mourning the Minnesota victims based on political alignment. This echoes the dystopian pacification in Huxley's Brave New World, where shallow distractions dull moral agency, but here, the thrill is the gladiatorial rush of cheering death as a tribal victory. The muted response to the Minnesota shootings, compared to the polarized outrage over Trump and Kirk, reveals a selective empathy that further fragments communal bonds, as reported in 2024–2025 analyses of rising political violence, with over 80,000 global protest incidents and nearly 9,500 threats against U.S. lawmakers investigated by the U.S. Capitol Police.

The irony is profound and tragic: those who decry fascism while advocating violence unwittingly embody its core tenets. Antifa and similar groups, claiming to combat authoritarianism, often employ tactics that echo the very ideology they oppose. As Benito Mussolini articulated in The Doctrine of Fascism (1932), fascism explicitly endorses political struggle and violence as vital to national vitality: "War alone brings up to its highest tension all human energy and puts the stamp of nobility upon the peoples who have the courage to meet it." This exaltation of conflict as a path to renewal reveals fascism's rejection of pacifism and its embrace of force as a moral imperative, a philosophy that, in practice, justifies intimidation, riots, and assaults on dissenting voices. Yet, in 2025's cultural landscape, calls for violence against conservatives like Kirk or Trump are framed as anti-fascist resistance, a self-deceptive inversion that accelerates societal fragmentation. This hypocrisy, rooted in nominalism's denial of universal morals (as traced in Chapter 2), allows individuals to rationalize brutality while ignoring Scripture's command to "love your enemies" (Matthew 5:44).

From a Christian perspective, this justification of violence signals a spiritual crisis, where the imago Dei, the divine image in every person (Genesis 1:27), is profaned. The Early Church, facing Roman persecution, responded not with vengeance but with prayer and witness, as in Acts 7:60, where Stephen prayed for his persecutors. In contrast, today's cultural rot fosters a gladiatorial mindset, amplified by social media's dopamine-driven outrage cycles, where cheering death becomes a badge of tribal loyalty. This echoes Huxley's Brave New World, where pacified masses trade moral agency for sensory thrills, but here, the thrill is the vicarious rush of violence. To counter this, classical education must revive the discernment to recognize such inversions, equipping believers to expose and resist them through reasoned apologetics and communal piety.

Ultimately, this rot underscores the urgency of renewal: without reclaiming folk culture's empathy and high culture's ethical elevation, society risks descending into barbarism, where life is expendable and violence is virtue.

The Predator's Paradise: When Justice Collapses, Society Follows

The cultural rot that cheers political assassinations is the same rot that allows rapists and murderers to walk free while farmers are jailed for raw milk sales or parents prosecuted for "misgendering" their child. This is not anomaly—it is design.

In 2025, 63% of Americans believe the justice system is "broken" (Gallup), with 78% of Gen Z saying it "protects the powerful" (Pew, 2025). The Epstein case is the archetype: a man who trafficked children for the elite, given a slap on the wrist in 2008, while whistleblowers like Edward Snowden face life in exile.

This inversion demoralizes the folk community. When a rapist serves less time than a marijuana dealer, the social contract frays. The high ideal of justice (Plato's *Republic*, Aquinas's *Summa*) is replaced by therapeutic utilitarianism: "rehabilitate the predator, punish the dissenter." The result? Vigilantism rises—as seen in X threads celebrating Kirk's murder or Trump's near-assassination. When the state fails to protect the innocent, the folk take justice into their own hands.

From a Christian view, this is Romans 1:32 in action: a society that "approves of those who practice" evil while condemning the righteous. The early church faced Nero's leniency toward gladiatorial murder but crucified Christians for refusing incense. Today, we crucify the truth-teller and coddle the predator.

Elite Corruption and the Distraction of Pop Culture

The rootlessness of a culture adrift creates fertile ground for elite corruption, as shallow pop culture distracts from systemic failures. The 1MDB scandal serves as a stark example: a $4.5 billion heist from Malaysia's sovereign wealth fund, orchestrated by financier Jho Low and enabled by Goldman Sachs, which funneled funds into Hollywood spectacles like The Wolf of Wall Street and elite luxuries, as revealed in 2025's ongoing trials and asset seizures. Media coverage often glamorized Low's lavish lifestyle, sidelining calls for systemic banking reform, a pattern enabled by a society distracted by pop culture's overdose. Online posts in 2024–2025 criticized mainstream outlets for downplaying 1MDB's ties to global elites, noting how blockbusters and viral social media divert attention from such injustices. This mirrors Huxley's vision of a populace too entertained to question power, a dynamic exacerbated by the decline of classical education, which once equipped individuals to discern truth and hold leaders accountable.

Corporate-driven pop culture plays a central role in this distraction. As noted earlier in discussions of franchise dilutions, this extends to emerging threats like AI-driven content, which risks dehumanizing human creativity and relationships. Christian scholars in 2025 warn that AI's capabilities, while innovative, lure individuals into surrendering agency, replacing authentic spiritual discernment with algorithmic outputs. For instance, AI chatbots posing as spiritual advisors could erode the relational core of discipleship, perverting the imago Dei (Genesis 1:27) by commodifying human souls. This dehumanization aligns with dystopian warnings of a society where technology supplants divine purpose, fostering corruption by detaching individuals from ethical accountability.

The corporate-government nexus amplifies this threat. Government policies that produce citizens less capable of critical inquiry. The removal of classical literature from school curricula, such as To Kill a Mockingbird or The Great Gatsby in various U.S. districts (e.g., Florida's 2023–2024 bans of over 700 books), limits exposure to narratives that challenge moral and intellectual growth. Meanwhile, economic policies like the 2008 TARP bailouts ($700 billion to banks) and 2020 COVID-19 relief, favoring large corporations over small businesses, entrench corporate dominance, and undermine the principled creators who might resist cultural homogenization. This creates a feedback loop: a less-educated populace, distracted by shallow pop culture, is less likely to demand accountability from elites, allowing corruption to flourish.

The Dystopian Vision: A Society Under Control

The culmination of cultural loss is a dystopian society where corporate and government interests dominate, leveraging pop culture and weakened education to maintain control. Orwell's 1984 depicts a world where history is rewritten to serve the state, a parallel to modern trends where cultural heritage is sidelined for corporate narratives. The decline of cursive writing instruction, removed from Common Core in 2010, isolates students from historical documents like the U.S. Constitution, weakening their connection to civic roots. While states like California are reinstating cursive, the gap has already eroded historical literacy. Similarly, the reduced emphasis on civic rituals like the national anthem in schools, stemming from controversies and legal precedents such as West Virginia State Board of Education v. Barnette (1943), diminishes shared folk traditions that once fostered unity.

Huxley's Brave New World offers another lens: a society pacified by entertainment and conditioned to accept superficiality. Today's algorithm-driven platforms, like Netflix or TikTok, mirror this by curating content that maximizes engagement through emotional manipulation rather than intellectual depth. Netflix's The Kissing Booth series (2018–2021) or TikTok's viral dance trends prioritize instant gratification over the layered narratives of classics like Shakespeare's Hamlet or Homer's Odyssey, which invite reflection across generations. A 2023 study by the University of

Southern California found that 70% of Gen Z consumers consume media primarily through algorithm-driven platforms, spending an average of 3.5 hours daily on short-form content that rarely fosters critical thinking. This conditions users to accept shallow narratives, making them more susceptible to corporate and government agendas.

The dystopian risk extends to surveillance and data manipulation. Edward Snowden's 2013 revelations about the NSA's PRISM program exposed government partnerships with tech giants like Google and Apple, collecting user data under the guise of security. The result is a society where individuals are monitored and manipulated, their preferences shaped by algorithms and their heritage replaced by corporate content, paving the way for a controlled, homogenized culture.

The Panopticon of Politeness: Corporate Therapeutic Tyranny and the Death of Private Life

In the dystopian trajectory traced throughout this chapter—rootlessness, moral rot, elite corruption, and the pacification of the masses—one of the most insidious mechanisms of control is the **total colonization of private speech** by corporate therapeutic ideology. What began as workplace "sensitivity training" in the 1990s has metastasized into a **surveillance state of the soul**, where every casual remark, every off-hand joke, every whispered conversation in a break room or private text thread carries the potential for social execution. This is not merely "political correctness"; it is **corporate Newspeak enforced by digital Stasi**, a regime in which human resources departments, DEI consultants, and anonymous reporting apps function as the new secret police of the therapeutic age.

Orwell warned that the ultimate goal of totalitarianism is to make rebellion *unthinkable* by making certain thoughts *unsayable.* In 2025, we are living that nightmare—not through crude state censorship (though that is coming), but through the velvet-gloved tyranny of **corporate politeness**. The average American now changes jobs every 4.1 years (U.S. Bureau of Labor Statistics, 2025), meaning most adults will face **at least twelve separate corporate loyalty oaths** to ever-shifting speech codes in their working lives. Each new employee handbook is a new catechism: thou shalt not misgender, thou shalt not deadname, thou shalt affirm every lifestyle, thou shalt signal enthusiasm for the latest ESG cause or risk being flagged as "not a culture fit."

The data are chilling. The Foundation for Individual Rights and Expression (FIRE) documented **1,827 sanctioned speech incidents** on U.S. campuses and workplaces in 2024 alone, with 68% originating from anonymous bias-reporting systems. In corporate America, the numbers are worse. A 2025 Cato Institute survey found that **62% of Americans**—and **74% of those under 30**—say they **self-censor** political or social opinions at work out of fear of retaliation. Among conservatives, the figure rises to **88%**. A separate Harvard/Harris poll in January 2025 revealed that **41% of registered voters** would support firing someone for privately held views on transgender issues, abortion, or race—even if those views never affected job performance. This is not protection of the vulnerable; this is **ritual purity testing** disguised as compassion.

The mechanism is deliberate. Modern HR software—Workday, BambooHR, Culture Amp—now includes **"sentiment analysis" tools** that scrape Slack messages, Microsoft Teams chats, and even private WhatsApp groups if synced to company devices. One wrong emoji, one skeptical meme, one "I'm not sure about that" in a diversity training Zoom can trigger an automated flag. The result? A **climate of omnipresent surveillance** where employees police their own thoughts before they reach their tongues. As one anonymous Google engineer wrote on X in March 2025 before being fired: *"We don't need Big Brother when we have Little Sister in HR."*

This therapeutic tyranny has **three dystopian effects** that directly accelerate the cultural loss described in this chapter:

1. **The annihilation of private life** Jürgen Habermas once described the bourgeois public sphere as sustained by a sharp distinction between public and private realms. That distinction is dead. In 2025, **private life is now auditable**. Leaked group chats, old tweets from age 14, even family dinner conversations recorded on a teenager's phone can be weaponized years later. The New York Times reported in June 2025 that **28% of Gen Z job applicants** were rejected after employers demanded access to private social media accounts—a practice courts have upheld under "at-will" employment. This is not background checking; it is **moral archaeology**, digging through digital strata to find any trace of ideological impurity.

2. **The enforced fragility of the public square** The therapeutic regime demands that every space be a "safe space," which in practice means **no space is allowed to be challenging**. Comedy clubs now require trigger warnings. Stand-up specials on Netflix carry content advisories for "mature themes" that would have been mild in 1995. Even churches are not immune: a 2025 Lifeway Research survey found that **34% of evangelical pastors**

have been pressured by congregants to avoid sermons on hell, sexual ethics, or gender roles lest they "traumatize" attendees. The result is a **culture of enforced fragility** where adults are treated as emotional infants, incapable of hearing disagreement without institutional protection. This is the mirror image of Huxley's soma-dosed citizens: instead of drugging pain away, we **ban the sources of pain**—which are, inevitably, other human beings with different views.

3. **The creation of a new clerical class: the therapeutic elite** Who enforces this regime? A **priestly caste of DEI officers, sensitivity readers, and corporate therapists** whose salaries now rival C-suite executives. At Fortune 500 companies, the average Chief Diversity Officer earns **$217,000** plus bonuses (Glassdoor, 2025), often more than the Chief Financial Officer. These are not elected positions. They are **unaccountable mandarins** who wield the power to end livelihoods with a single email. As Christopher Rufo documented in his 2025 exposé *The New Commissars*, many of these officers have no background in law, theology, or philosophy—only in **activist training programs** that teach conflict as trauma and disagreement as violence. Their creed is simple: **comfort is justice, discomfort is harm**.

From a Christian perspective, this therapeutic tyranny is a **demonic inversion** of the Gospel. Where Christ called believers to "speak the truth in love" (Ephesians 4:15) and to bear with one another's weaknesses, the new regime demands **speech that causes no discomfort whatsoever**—a standard no human relationship can meet. Where the early church faced Roman persecution for proclaiming Christ crucified, modern believers face **corporate persecution for refusing to proclaim the new dogmas**. The Book of Revelation speaks of a time when "no one can buy or sell" without the mark of the beast (Rev 13:17). In 2025, that mark is not a microchip—it is the **perfectly curated LinkedIn profile**, the **pronouns in bio**, the **Black Lives Matter banner on the Slack status**. Refuse to signal, and you are excommunicated from economic life.

Yet cracks are appearing. The **post-liberal Gen Z backlash** documented earlier in this chapter is accelerating. On X, TikTok, and private Discords, young men especially are rediscovering **unapologetic speech**—sharing 90s stand-up clips, posting "incorrect" memes, and openly mocking corporate virtue scripts. A 2025 Barna study found that **58% of Gen Z Christians** now say they would rather lose a job than violate their conscience on cultural issues—up from 41% in 2022. Underground comedy scenes in Los Angeles, Austin, and Miami are selling out 500-seat venues with comics who refuse to self-censor. Indie creators on Substack and Rumble are earning six figures telling jokes that would get them fired from Netflix tomorrow.

This is the **folk culture response** to therapeutic tyranny: raw, irreverent, human. It is the modern equivalent of the medieval carnival—moments when the social order is inverted, hierarchies mocked, and the powerful reminded that they rule only by consent. As Kierkegaard's knight of faith stood alone against the crowd, these young rebels are making the **absurd leap** of speaking freely in a world that punishes truth. Their courage is not merely cultural—it is **prophetic**.

The renewal this chapter calls for must therefore include a **radical reclamation of private speech**. Classical education must teach not only logic and rhetoric but **comic courage**—the ability to laugh at power, to speak truth without fear, to bear the cost of nonconformity. Churches must become **sanctuaries of unfiltered conversation**, where members can confess doubts, voice frustrations, and debate Scripture without fear of being reported to HR (or the pastor's wife). Homes must be **fortresses of candor**, where children learn that words are not violence and disagreement is not hate.

Until we restore the right to **whisper heresy in the break room**, the dystopian future warned of in this chapter is not coming—it is already here. But the same God who confused the tongues at Babel can loose them again. The therapeutic empire, like all Babylon's, will fall. And when it does, the first sound will be **unrestrained human laughter**—the folk culture's ancient weapon against tyranny, and the surest sign that the image of God in man has not been finally silenced.

Theological Echoes of Dystopia: Judgment and Hope

From a Christian perspective, this cultural loss and dystopian trajectory reflect a spiritual crisis, where the rejection of God's truth for materialistic idols leads to moral and societal decay. Karl Barth's *Church Dogmatics* (Vol. IV/3) diagnoses societal fragmentation as humanity's estrangement from God's covenant, a "rush into the void" without Christ's reconciliation. This theological view frames modern rootlessness, evident in Gen Z's spiritual nomadism, as a covenantal breach, per Ephesians 2:12, in which individuals become "strangers to the promises" amid digital isolation. Yet, Barth's emphasis on reconciliation offers hope: cultural renewal begins with restoring covenantal communities through the church.

Dietrich Bonhoeffer's *Life Together* (1939) further illuminates this, warning of "spiritual homelessness" where cultural distractions foster cheap grace without discipleship. In 2025's context of ideology supplanting theology, such as political dogmas overshadowing doctrine, Bonhoeffer's critique urges Christians to prioritize authentic community over ideological dreams. N.T. Wright's *Surprised by Hope* (2008, with 2024 reflections) adds eschatological depth, viewing dystopias as "foretastes of judgment" but harbingers of new creation (2 Corinthians 5:17), where resurrection reaffirms creation's goodness against dehumanizing forces like AI. Timothy Keller's *Hope in Times of Fear* (2021) addresses contemporary fragility, noting how secular performance-based identities amplify fear, per Psalm 146:3-5, calling believers to anchor in God's help amid elite manipulations.

Echoing these voices, the Danish Lutheran philosopher Søren Kierkegaard (1813–1855) offers a piercing, ironic critique of "Christendom," that complacent, institutionalized form of Christianity where subjective faith devolves into superficial conformity, stripping the individual of the absurd, existential leap required for true encounter with the divine. In *Fear and Trembling* (1843), Kierkegaard pseudonymously explores the biblical story of Abraham's near-sacrifice of Isaac (Genesis 22) through the lens of the "knight of faith," a figure who embraces the absurd: God's command defies ethical reason, demanding a silent, subjective obedience that isolates the believer from societal norms and rational assurance. This is no mere theological exercise but a radical confrontation with faith's paradoxes, how the eternal irrupts into the temporal, forcing the individual to suspend the universal (ethical duty) for the absolute (divine telos). Kierkegaard lambasts "Christendom" for its bourgeois complacency, where the church becomes a cultural club, peddling objective doctrines without the subjective passion that turns belief into existential risk. As he writes under the pseudonym Johannes de Silentio:

"Faith is precisely the paradox that the single individual as the single individual is higher than the universal... the single individual as the single individual stands in an absolute relation to the absolute."

In our dystopian age of 2025, Kierkegaard's diagnosis resonates profoundly with the rootlessness traced earlier in this chapter: a society pacified by algorithmic pop culture and secular ideologies mirrors the "Christendom" of his day, where faith is reduced to comfortable rituals Sunday services streamed on TikTok, or political alliances masquerading as piety devoid of the absurd leap that demands personal sacrifice amid cultural decay. The Epstein scandals and corporate bailouts thrive in this numbness, as a complacent church, echoing nominalism's subjective relativism (Chapter 2), fails to call believers to the knight of faith's isolation: standing alone before God, rejecting the herd's distractions for radical trust. Yet, Kierkegaard's irony is not despairing but provocative, a call to subjective depth that pierces the heart, urging individuals to reclaim faith's absurdity as resistance. In a world of shallow distractions, this leap becomes a bulwark against Huxley's pacified masses, fostering resilient souls who, like Abraham, wager everything on the divine amid the void. As Kierkegaard implies, true renewal begins not in institutional reform but in the single individual's defiant, hopeful obedience, a Lutheran echo that bridges personal piety to communal revival, pointing toward the eschatological hope Wright envisions.

Fresh Horizons: Eschatology, Generations, and Global Witness

An eschatological perspective reframes dystopia as a divine invitation to renewal, drawing from Revelation's apocalyptic imagery. The fall of Babylon (Revelation 18) symbolizes materialistic empires' collapse, mirroring today's corporate homogenization, yet promising restoration for the faithful. This lens encourages active participation in societal healing, such as ethical advocacy against surveillance, embodying "living water" (John 7:38) in arid cultural landscapes.

Generationally, Gen Z faces unique challenges like "disjointed theology" and secular pressures, with 49% identifying as "nones" and only 38% as Christians in 2025 surveys. Yet, trends show spiritual openness among teens, with men returning to church at higher rates, signaling potential revival if addressed through folk-high integration. Globally, while Western Christianity shrinks, Lifeway Research's 2025 trends highlight encouragement: Christianity grows at 1.27% annually, nones have plateaued, and atheism declines, driven by Evangelical surges in Africa and Asia. This resilience blending indigenous worship with doctrinal depth offers models for Western renewal, countering secular theocracies where ideologies mimic religion, as critiqued in Christian readings of Huxley's World State as a "dystopian secular theocracy."

Amid these generational challenges, the rise of non-denominationalism emerges as a particularly insidious contributor to the "disjointed theology" plaguing Gen Z, often exacerbating rather than alleviating the spiritual void left by cultural erosion. Non-denominational churches, which have proliferated in the West since the late 20th century, now comprise over 20% of U.S. “Protestant” congregations according to the 2020 Faith Communities Today survey, with projections of further growth in 2025 frequently prioritizing contemporary appeal over historical continuity, severing believers from the rich tapestry of church history that once anchored faith in communal and transcendent truths. This disconnection manifests in worship styles that eschew the liturgical depth of ancient creeds, patristic writings, and sacramental traditions, opting instead for seeker-friendly formats that emphasize emotional experience and personal relevance. While intended to attract the spiritually nomadic, this approach dilutes theological rigor, leaving congregants without the intellectual scaffolding whose works integrated folk wisdom with high doctrinal precision to foster resilient faith communities.

Compounding this is the often feminized character of non-denominational environments, which, through an emphasis on relational softness, emotive worship music, and therapeutic sermons, can inadvertently alienate men and young boys seeking models of robust spiritual leadership and moral fortitude. Surveys from the Barna Group in 2024 indicate that male attendance in non-denominational settings lags behind women by 15-20%, with many men reporting a sense of disconnection from the "masculine virtues" of discipline, sacrifice, and accountability extolled in Scripture (e.g., 1 Corinthians 16:13: "Be on your guard; stand firm in the faith; be courageous; be strong"). This feminization, while not inherently negative in balanced contexts, risks stunting the holistic development of young males in a society already grappling with identity fragmentation, as boys grow up without the objective beauty of structured rites such as the solemnity of Gregorian chants or the architectural grandeur of Gothic cathedrals that historically inspired awe and aspiration toward divine order. Instead, non-denominational spaces often favor minimalist aesthetics and subjective expressions, echoing nominalism's rejection of universal beauty (Chapter 2) and contributing to the aesthetic poverty that leaves souls unmoored.

Furthermore, the lack of theological accountability in many non-denominational structures devoid of denominational oversight, confessional standards, or historical councils fosters a relativistic ethos where doctrine bends to cultural trends, mirroring the pop culture distractions critiqued throughout this chapter. Without the checks of ecumenical creeds like the Nicene or Apostles' Creed, pastors and congregants risk drifting into "disjointed theology," where personal interpretation supplants communal discernment, amplifying the rootlessness. This vulnerability is evident in 2025 Online discussions on "non-denominational pitfalls," where users lament doctrinal inconsistencies and leadership scandals, such as unaddressed financial improprieties or watered-down teachings on sin and redemption. From a Christian perspective, this echoes Kierkegaard's critique of complacent "Christendom," where faith devolves into superficial conformity without the absurd leap of existential commitment. Yet, as Gen Z pivots toward traditionalism with rising interest in Catholic, Orthodox, and confessional Protestant forms, per Pew's 2025 Youth Faith Survey this trend offers hope: by reclaiming denominational roots that integrate church history, theological depth, and objective beauty, young believers can resist feminized shallowness and embrace accountable communities that nurture men and boys in strong, responsible and educated individuals.

The Potential of Pop Culture Done Right

Pop culture, when not weaponized, can harmonize folk and high culture, offering a glimpse of what's possible. Vernor Vinge's A Fire Upon the Deep (1992) blends folk-inspired narratives gritty tales of medieval pack-minds on a Tines world, wrestling with loyalty, betrayal, and primal survival akin to saga cycles with high philosophical explorations of distributed intelligence, the limits of cognition, and the ethics of godlike transcendences, echoing Christian themes of providence and redemption found in Bunyan's The Pilgrim's Progress. Its creator, driven by scientific imagination over market formulas, crafted a universe that resonates globally, earning praise for its "prophetic depth" in a landscape of shallow content. Similarly, Denis Villeneuve's Dune (2021) retained Frank Herbert's complex themes of ecology, religion, and power, balancing folk-inspired world-building with high philosophical inquiry. These successes show that pop culture can bridge communal grounding and intellectual elevation, but only when crafted with purpose rather than profit.

In contrast, corporate weaponization through algorithms, merchandising, or narrative simplification undermines this potential. The Marvel Cinematic Universe (MCU), for instance, has shifted from standalone stories like Iron Man (2008), with its exploration of responsibility, to formulaic sequels prioritizing interconnected merchandising over depth. Fan critiques highlight this, noting how recent MCU films feel like "assembly-line products" compared to earlier entries' moral weight. These examples underscore how corporate priorities erode pop culture's capacity to inspire, pushing society toward dystopian shallowness.

Historical Precedents for Resistance

History offers hope through examples of resistance to cultural decline. The American Founding Fathers, rooted in classical education, saw an educated populace as essential for liberty. Thomas Jefferson, in a 1816 letter to Charles Yancey, wrote, "If a nation expects to be ignorant and free, in a state of civilization, it expects what never was and never will be." His love for books, evidenced by his 6,487-volume library donated to form the Library of Congress, informed a vision of citizens equipped to challenge tyranny through knowledge of folk traditions (like colonial ballads) and high philosophical ideals (from Locke and Montesquieu). John Adams echoed this in 1765, stating, "Liberty cannot be preserved without a general knowledge among the people."

By equipping believers to read the Bible and engage with cultural heritage, Luther fostered a movement that challenged centralized power, fostering accountability and reform. Similarly, the medieval York Mystery Plays (14th–16th centuries) united folk traditions with theological depth, strengthening communal piety against moral decay.

The Erosion of High Culture: Financial Struggles and the Loss of Objective Beauty in the West

The rootlessness of a culture adrift, as explored earlier in this chapter, extends beyond the fragmentation of communal identity to the very institutions that once elevated society through high culture, those bastions of objective beauty, proportion, and integrity that Aquinas so eloquently described in his *Summa Theologica* as reflections of the Creator's harmony. In the United States and broader Western world, high culture is facing existential threats, not merely from the algorithmic distractions of pop culture but from systemic financial pressures that mirror the materialistic ethos critiqued in Chapter 3. Opera houses, symphonies, and traditional arts venues, emblems of the folk-high synergy that once bound communities in shared aspiration, are closing, downsizing, or turning to desperate measures for survival. This decline, exacerbated by government funding cuts and declining attendance, signals a deeper spiritual void: the replacement of transcendent, Christian-infused art with subjective, relativistic expressions that echo nominalism's denial of universal truths (as traced in Chapter 2). Far from enriching the soul, these shifts produce a society increasingly disconnected from the eternal verities that foster moral conviction and communal bonds, paving the way for the centralized control warned of in Huxley's *Brave New World.*

In the United States, the opera industry, a pinnacle of high culture blending dramatic narrative, musical depth, and visual splendor, exemplifies this peril. The Metropolitan Opera (Met) in New York, the nation's largest performing arts organization, reported an operating deficit exceeding $50 million for the 2024-25 season, leading to a second credit downgrade to a highly speculative B- rating by Moody's in August 2025. This follows persistent post-pandemic struggles, with expenses significantly outpacing revenue amid dwindling ticket sales and philanthropy. The Met has resorted to unconventional partnerships, such as a lucrative deal announced in September 2025 to perform three weeks annually at Saudi Arabia's $1.4 billion Royal Diriyah Opera House starting in 2028, staging works like Mozart's *The Magic Flute* and Puccini's *La Bohème* during its winter break. While this may provide short-term relief, it underscores the desperation of an industry once sustained by domestic cultural patronage, now compelled to seek foreign shores for viability.

Smaller companies fare even worse. Detroit Opera canceled its 2025-26 season opener, Puccini's *The Girl of the Golden West*, in July 2025 due to a $3 million shortfall from diminished grants, donations, and ticket sales, amid broader industry inflation and economic recession. On Site Opera, an innovative New York-based ensemble founded in 2012, shuttered entirely in January 2025, citing a 50% rise in production costs since the pandemic and dwindling government contributions. These closures are not isolated; OPERA America's 2024 Annual Field Report reveals a sector-wide crisis, with U.S. opera companies facing revenue volatility, rising administrative expenses, and thin margins, compounded by demographic shifts like declining migration to arts-rich urban areas. Federal funding cuts from the National Endowment for the Arts (NEA) have accelerated this erosion: in

May 2025, hundreds of grants were abruptly canceled, including those supporting opera and cultural preservation, as the Trump administration proposed eliminating the NEA entirely. State-level appropriations for arts are projected to drop 10% in fiscal year 2025, leaving institutions like the Berkeley Repertory Theater and Chicago's Open Studio Project scrambling to replace lost funds.

Attendance trends paint an equally grim picture. According to the National Endowment for the Arts' Survey of Public Participation in the Arts, only 4.6% of U.S. adults attended a classical music performance in 2022, a statistically significant decline from pre-pandemic levels and a continuation of a decades-long downward trajectory down nearly 4% from 1982 to 2008, with further drops among younger demographics and ethnic minorities. In Europe, similar patterns emerge. Classical music concert attendance has stagnated or fallen amid economic pressures, with the UK seeing A-level music entries hit a historic low in 2025 after 15 years of decline, signaling a shrinking pipeline of future audiences and performers. Berlin's December 2024 decision to slash its culture budget by €130 million (12%) for 2025 despite protests has forced museums like the KW Institute for Contemporary Art to cut programs and staff, threatening the city's status as a cultural hub.

Compounding these financial woes is the spiritual dimension: the loss of Christian art's objective beauty to subjective, relativistic expressions that dominate modern galleries. For centuries, Christian art from Byzantine icons to Renaissance masterpieces like Michelangelo’s Sistine Chapel served as a visual theology, embodying Hans Urs von Balthasar’s theological aesthetics by ordering human affections toward divine harmony and truth (Psalm 19:1). These works, with their clarity and proportion, mirrored God’s creation and invited contemplation of eternal realities, bridging folk narratives (e.g., biblical parables) with high philosophical depth. Yet, as nominalism's legacy took hold (Chapter 2), art shifted toward subjectivity, where "beauty is in the eye of the beholder" became a mantra that severed aesthetics from transcendent anchors.

In contemporary Western culture, this manifests as a decline in Christian-themed art, replaced by abstract or conceptual works that prioritize personal whim over universal virtue. Church patronage, once a fountain of inspiration, has waned since the 18th century's secular revolutions, leading to sterile, utilitarian church decorations and a broader "defiant attitude towards art and culture" in Protestant circles. Modern galleries favor relativistic pieces, e.g., conceptual installations devoid of narrative or beauty that critique institutions like the Church without offering a redemptive vision, reflecting a "spiritual homelessness" Bonhoeffer warned of in *Life Together* (Chapter 6). As theologian David Brown argues, human culture, including the visual arts, is a site of religious experience that is often neglected today, resulting in an "anticulture" in which art no longer points to God but indulges in subjective isolation. Funding cuts exacerbate this: NEA and NEH rescissions in 2025 have disproportionately hit programs supporting diverse or faith-based arts, forcing Christian artists to the margins while subjective works thrive in a market-driven ecosystem.

This erosion of high culture is no mere economic footnote; it is a dystopian harbinger. As Martin Luther warned in his 1524 To the Councilmen of All Cities in Germany That They Establish and Maintain Christian Schools, "If we let the languages go, we shall not only lose the Gospel, but it will finally come to pass that we shall not be able to speak or write correct Latin or German" a prophecy of cultural and spiritual barrenness where the arts, once bearers of divine truth, wither into silence. In a West where opera houses shutter and Christian art fades, society trades the garden of transcendent harmony for Huxley's pacified shadows, where shallow distractions reign and elite corruption evades scrutiny.

The Slow Decline of Folk Culture: Rising Costs and Aging Demographics

While high culture institutions like opera houses grapple with existential financial crises, as detailed above, folk culture events rooted in communal traditions and accessible narratives fare somewhat better in terms of popularity and resilience. Medieval festivals (often manifested as Renaissance faires) and colonial-era reenactments, which embody the earthy wisdom of folk heritage discussed in Chapter 4, attract larger crowds and foster a sense of shared identity through immersive experiences like jousting, artisan crafts, and historical role-playing. These events, drawing from Celtic lays, Germanic legends, and American colonial stories, once bridged generations, weaving community bonds in ways that counter the rootlessness of our materialistic age. Yet, even these vibrant expressions are not immune to decline. Rising operational costs, driven by inflation and post-pandemic recovery, combined with aging demographics and waning youth participation, signal a gradual erosion. If unchecked, this could lead to the long-term loss of these traditions, severing society from its folk roots and amplifying a dystopian isolation in which authentic communal experiences are supplanted by synthetic distractions.

In the United States, Renaissance fairs, modern evolutions of medieval festivals, remain a cultural staple, with dozens of events drawing millions annually. The Texas Renaissance Festival, one of the largest, hosted over 500,000 visitors in its 2024 season, featuring themed weekends, jousting, and artisan markets.

Similarly, the Maryland Renaissance Festival reported steady attendance of around 300,000 in 2024, blending historical reenactments with family-friendly entertainment. These figures suggest folk events outperform high culture counterparts; for instance, while the Metropolitan Opera struggles with deficits exceeding $50 million (as noted earlier), Renaissance fairs often operate on self-sustaining models through ticket sales and vendor fees. However, underlying trends reveal vulnerabilities. Operational costs have surged 20-30% since 2020 due to inflation in labor, materials, and insurance, forcing some fairs to raise admission prices. Adult tickets now average $25-35, up from $20-25 pre-pandemic, potentially pricing out families amid economic pressures.

Demographics further underscore a slow decline: participants and attendees are aging, with average ages skewing toward 40-60 years old, according to surveys from events like the Bristol Renaissance Faire and Pennsylvania Renaissance Faire. Youth participation, once a vibrant draw through interactive elements like knight training or fairy tales, has dipped; a 2023 study on small Texas faires found that while motivations include escapism and education, younger demographics (18-34) represent only 25-30% of attendees, down from 35-40% a decade ago, citing competing digital entertainment and higher costs as barriers. X discussions in 2024-2025 highlight this: users lament "fewer kids at ren faires now, mostly boomers in costume," attributing it to social media's pull and economic hurdles like $10-15 child tickets plus travel expenses. If this trend continues, these festivals risk becoming relics, losing the intergenerational transmission of folk wisdom that Luther championed in his educational reforms (Chapter 1).

Colonial-era reenactments, particularly those commemorating the American Revolution, face similar headwinds, though they maintain cultural relevance amid the 250th anniversary celebrations in 2025-2026. Events like the Lexington reenactment in April 2025 drew thousands to witness the "shot heard round the world," with participants in period attire recreating battles and daily life, grounding audiences in the folk narratives of communal resistance and virtue. The Sons of the American Revolution (SAR) reported over 100 events nationwide in 2024, including youth-focused programs like living history camps. Attendance remains robust, e.g., the Gettysburg 155th anniversary in 2018 drew 15,000-20,000 reenactors, but recent data points to a decline. The Wall Street Journal's 2024 report on Revolutionary War reenactors notes shrinking groups: the Huntington Militia in New York has dwindled to 40 members (half active), down from 50 in 2013, with commanders struggling to recruit amid aging rosters (average age mid-50s) and youth disinterest.

Rising costs exacerbate this: outfitting for authenticity muskets, uniforms, tents can exceed $1,000 per participant, up 15-20% since 2020 due to supply chain issues, deterring newcomers. Youth participation has notably declined; the WSJ highlights groups turning to social media and YouTube for recruitment, as older members retire or pass away, with heatstroke and health issues (linked to aging) disrupting events. A 2023 SAR survey estimated only 10-15% of participants were under 30, down from 20-25% a decade ago, attributing it to competing activities like video games and economic barriers (event fees averaging $50-100). Globally, similar trends in Europe, e.g., UK historical societies reporting 10-15% membership drops post-pandemic, mirror this, with aging demographics threatening the transmission of folk traditions like colonial ballads or revolutionary reenactments that once inspired civic virtue (per Chapter 5's Founding Fathers discussion).

This slow fade of folk culture events, while less acute than high culture's collapse, portends a profound loss: without youth engagement, these traditions vital for countering materialism's "futile thinking" risk extinction, leaving society even more vulnerable to algorithmic pacification and elite manipulation. As Bonhoeffer's "spiritual homelessness" takes hold, the communal hearth of folk heritage dims, amplifying the dystopian trajectory. Yet, as Chapter 7 proposes, renewal through classical education and church-led initiatives, perhaps sponsoring youth scholarships for reenactments or integrating folk festivals into catechesis, can reverse this, reclaiming these events as bridges to transcendent truth and communal resilience.

Conclusion: A Call to Action

The dystopian consequences of cultural loss, rootlessness, elite corruption, and centralized control threaten to reshape society into a hollow reflection of its potential. Yet, the path to renewal lies within our grasp. By reviving classical education, rooted in Western Christian thought, we can restore the synergy of folk and high culture, equipping individuals to resist shallow pop culture and systemic corruption. This is not a nostalgic retreat but a forward-looking revolution, inspired by historical successes like the Reformation and the Founding Fathers' vision. As we explore in the next chapter, this renewal begins with practical steps within homes, churches, and schools to reclaim our cultural soul, ensuring that future generations inherit a society rich in meaning and resilient against dystopian decay.

Chapter 7: A Path Forward: Reclaiming Folk and High Culture and Reforming Governance

The dystopian consequences of cultural loss, rootlessness, vulnerability to manipulation, and elite corruption paint a grim picture, but they are not inevitable. As we've examined throughout this book, the decline of classical education and the overdose of weaponized pop culture have eroded the synergy of folk and high culture, fueling materialism and disconnecting society from its moral and intellectual roots. Yet, history offers a blueprint for renewal: reforms rooted in Western Christian thought, driven by academics, educators, and church leaders who integrated faith, reason, and virtue to counter decay. By reviving classical education, supporting the symbiotic relationship between folk and high culture, resisting pop culture's excesses, reforming governance through principled accountability, and drawing on a wealth of sources from Classical Protestant and broader Christian traditions, we can reclaim our heritage and build a society resilient against materialism. This path forward, inspired by figures like Martin Luther and contemporary scholars, emphasizes education not merely as knowledge acquisition but as a divine calling to form souls, shape young minds, and foster communal bonds that echo the eternal truths of Scripture. It is a call to action for homes, churches, schools, and communities to invest in legacies that transcend generations, ensuring that the true, the good, and the beautiful prevail over the shallow and the fleeting.

The Imperative of Christians in Academic Institutions

Central to this renewal is the urgent need for Christians to reclaim their presence and influence in academic institutions. For too long, secular ideologies have dominated universities and schools, sidelining the Christian worldview that once formed the bedrock of Western education. Christians in academia serve as guardians of truth, beauty, and virtue, integrating faith with rigorous scholarship to counter materialism and cultural downgrade. Their role is not merely defensive but transformative: by shaping curricula, mentoring students, and advancing research grounded in biblical principles, they equip future generations to discern truth amid relativism and to apply moral convictions to societal challenges. Without this presence, academia risks becoming an echo chamber of humanistic autonomy, as Francis Schaeffer warned, leading to further cultural fragmentation.

Contemporary exemplars illustrate this transformative potential, demonstrating how Christians in diverse fields can reclaim intellectual territory without compromising their witness. At MIT, Professor Ian Hutchinson, a pioneering nuclear scientist and head of the Plasma Science and Fusion Center, weaves empirical rigor with unapologetic faith, authoring *Can a Scientist Believe in Miracles?* (2018) to dismantle the myth of inevitable secularism in STEM. Hutchinson argues that objective inquiry far from contradicting miracles reveals a universe ordered by divine intentionality, echoing Aquinas's sacramental view of creation (*Summa Theologica*, I, q. 1, a. 5). His mentorship of graduate students, including seminars on faith-science integration, counters the materialistic reductionism that dominates elite labs, fostering a new generation equipped to engage cultural debates on AI ethics and bioengineering with biblical discernment rather than utilitarian drift.

In medicine and ethics, Columbia University's Associate Professor Lydia Dugdale exemplifies stewardship amid suffering, directing the Center for Clinical Medical Ethics while practicing palliative care. Dugdale draws on her faith to advocate for holistic healing that honors the *imago Dei* (Genesis 1:27), as detailed in her book *The Lost Art of Dying* (2021), which critiques modern medicine's denial of mortality and calls for rituals reclaiming death as a passage to eternal hope. During the COVID-19 crisis, she volunteered in overwhelmed wards, embodying Bonhoeffer's "costly grace" (*Life Together*, 1939) by prioritizing vulnerable lives over institutional efficiency. Her work reshapes curricula at Columbia's Vagelos College of Physicians and Surgeons, incorporating influential texts like John Wyatt's *Matters of Life and Death* alongside bioethics case studies, training physicians to resist the commodification of human dignity that fuels elite corruption and healthcare inequities.

Turning to philosophy, Alvin Plantinga, John A. O'Brien Professor of Philosophy Emeritus at Notre Dame, has fortified Christian epistemology against nominalist skepticism, proving faith's warrant in a post-Enlightenment academy. In *Warranted Christian Belief* (2000), Plantinga deploys Reformed epistemology to argue that belief in God is "properly basic," rationally justified without evidentialist proofs, directly challenging the relativism that undergirds shallow pop culture and cultural downgrade. His influence extends through mentoring figures like Nicholas Wolterstorff and shaping Notre Dame's Center for Philosophy of Religion, where seminars blend folk-like parables (e.g., Jesus' mustard seed, Matthew 13:31–32) with high analytic rigor, equipping scholars to defend objective truth in debates on AI-generated "realities" and ethical nominalism.

Finally, at Trinity Evangelical Divinity School, Research Professor of Systematic Theology Kevin J. Vanhoozer reimagines doctrine as dramatic performance, countering the performative superficiality of social media with a theology of faithful witness. In *The Drama of Doctrine* (2005), Vanhoozer casts the Christian life as a theo-drama, where believers improvise Scripture's script amid cultural improvisation, integrating folk narratives (e.g., Bunyan's allegorical pilgrimage) with high Augustinian depth to foster communicative virtue. His 2025 lectures on "Theodrama in a Post-Truth Age" address Gen Z's spiritual nomadism, urging seminarians to script resistance against algorithmic manipulation through ecclesial storytelling. Vanhoozer's approach revives the Trivium for theology grammar as scriptural literacy, logic as doctrinal discernment, rhetoric as confessional eloquence training pastors and scholars to perform truth in boardrooms and classrooms alike.

These figures, Hutchinson in science, Dugdale in ethics, Plantinga in philosophy, and Vanhoozer in theology, embody the guardian role, not as cultural warriors but as faithful stewards whose scholarship irrigates deserts of doubt. They remind us that Christian presence in academia is a divine commission: to "plunder the Egyptians" (Exodus 3:22), redeeming secular tools for Gospel ends, and to mentor the next wave of thinkers who will dismantle materialism's strongholds from within.

Historical Evidence: Classical Education Paving the Way for Christian Influence

History abounds with evidence of how classical education has enabled Christians to enter, build, and lead academies and churches, thereby shaping culture with lasting impact. Rooted in the ancient liberal arts of Greece and Rome, classical education was redeemed by early Christians like Saint Augustine, who in On Christian Doctrine advocated harnessing pagan learning for biblical exegesis and moral formation. This integration allowed Christians to establish cathedral schools and monasteries in the medieval era, which evolved into Europe's first universities: Bologna (1088), Oxford (1096), and Cambridge (1209), founded explicitly to train clergy and scholars in theology, philosophy, and the arts. These institutions blended folk traditions (local vernacular teachings) with high culture (Aristotelian logic and patristic theology), producing thinkers like Thomas Aquinas whose Summa Theologica synthesized reason and faith, influencing law, ethics, and governance for centuries.

The Protestant Reformation amplified this legacy. Martin Luther, himself classically educated in Latin, Greek, and Hebrew at Erfurt and Wittenberg, viewed education as essential for spiritual and civic renewal. In his 1524 treatise To the Councilmen of All Cities in Germany That They Establish and Maintain Christian Schools, Luther urged the establishment of public schools to teach classical languages alongside Scripture, enabling all boys and girls to read the Bible independently and resist ecclesiastical corruption. This led to a proliferation of Protestant academies across Europe, such as the University of Marburg (1527) and Geneva Academy (1559) under John Calvin, which trained pastors and reformers who spread the Gospel and reformed societies. These institutions shaped culture by producing hymnals, catechisms, and vernacular literature that merged folk piety with high theological depth, fostering resilient communities that withstood persecution and secular pressures.

In America, classical education paved the way for Christian-founded colleges that profoundly influenced the nation's founding. Harvard (1636), established to train Puritan ministers, adopted a classical curriculum emphasizing Latin, Greek, logic, and rhetoric, grounded in Christian doctrine. Similarly, Yale (1701) and Princeton (1746) were created to counter secular drifts in education, producing leaders like Jonathan Edwards whose revivalist preaching blended classical rhetoric with folk evangelism, sparking the Great Awakening and embedding Christian values in American culture. These academies equipped the Founding Fathers, many of whom were classically educated at such institutions, with moral convictions to ground the Republic in enduring principles, as discussed in previous chapters. Figures like Thomas Jefferson and John Adams drew on classical Christian thought to craft documents like the Declaration of Independence, ensuring long-term stability through systems rooted in virtue and natural law.

This historical pattern demonstrates that classical education empowers Christians to build institutions that outlast immediate crises, shaping culture through generations. The modern resurgence of classical Christian schools, with enrollment projected to reach 1.4 million by 2035 and a market exceeding $10 billion, echoes this legacy, producing students who outperform peers in critical thinking and civic engagement.

Acknowledging Populism's Efforts While Critiquing Its Shortcomings

While populism has played a role in mobilizing grassroots movements and challenging elite corruption efforts worthy of acknowledgment, its inherent strain of anti-intellectualism renders it short-sighted and incapable of fostering long-term prosperity or change. Populism often appeals to common sense and direct action, as seen in historical movements like Jacksonian democracy or modern expressions against globalism, which have amplified voices marginalized by corporate-government nexuses. However, by dismissing advanced scholarship as elitist, populism undermines the rigorous thinking needed to build enduring systems. Critics note that populist rhetoric primes anti-intellectual predispositions, fostering suspicion of experts and complex ideas, which erodes the church's ability to engage culture deeply. In the church, this manifests as neglect of apologetics and theology, reducing faith to emotionalism rather than reasoned conviction, as lamented by thinkers like J.P. Moreland in Love Your God with All Your Mind.

This anti-intellectualism is short-sighted because true, lasting change requires academic elites with moral convictions to institutionalize reforms, as evidenced by the Reformation and American founding. Without this, populism devolves into fleeting protests, failing to construct academies, churches, or governance structures that endure. The church must adopt long-term thinking, investing in classical education to produce leaders who ground movements in sustainable systems, echoing the Founding Fathers' reliance on classically trained minds to establish a republic that has lasted over two centuries.

The tide of populism, with its vigor in challenging the unaccountable, whether the veiled networks of Epstein's scandals or the $700 billion TARP bailouts, deserves acknowledgment for amplifying the voice of the overlooked. Yet, its strain of anti-intellectualism, casting scholarship as aloof or elitist, sows a fleeting harvest, incapable of the enduring renewal our culture craves. Far from a tarnished term, "elite" rightly denotes those called to lead as shepherds of the mind, guiding with moral clarity rather than grasping for selfish gain. The corruption that taints some of those who wield influence like a merchant's coin, hoarding power as in the shadows of Epstein's era, distorts their true calling: to steward wisdom for the common good, as Augustine's *ordo amoris* bids us order our loves toward God and neighbor. Populism's suspicion of rigorous thought risks reducing faith to mere sentiment, as J.P. Moreland laments in *Love Your God with All Your Mind*: "The church's neglect of apologetics and theology leaves us defenseless against a secular age."

True and lasting change, as history attests, springs not from fervor alone but from minds honed by classical education and anchored in Christian virtue. Martin Luther, in his 1524 treatise, urged schools to cultivate such leaders, men and women versed in Scripture and the liberal arts, capable of reforming church and state with wisdom, not merely passion. The Reformation's academies, like Wittenberg and Geneva, birthed elites who blended folk piety with high theology, crafting hymnals and catechisms that endured centuries. Similarly, America's Founding Fathers, educated in the classics at Harvard and Princeton, forged a republic grounded in moral conviction, as John Adams declared: "Liberty cannot be preserved without a general knowledge among the people." Today, the resurgence of classical Christian schools, projected to educate 1.4 million by 2035 in a $10 billion market, echoes this legacy, training students to lead with discernment, not disdain for learning

Transcending the Football Team Mentality: Beyond Republican vs. Democrat

The cultural and political challenges we face cannot be reduced to a simplistic Republican-versus-Democrat dichotomy, as this "football team mentality" fosters division and distracts from the deeper issue: who controls the institutions that shape society's values. The problem is not merely which party holds power but who wields influence within academia, media, education, and governance, shaping culture for generations. James Davison Hunter's *To Change the World* (2010) critiques the church's tendency to align with partisan camps, arguing that such alliances trade long-term cultural influence for short-term political wins. Instead, Hunter advocates for "faithful presence" Christians embedding themselves in institutions to renew them from within through virtuous example, not partisan conquest. This approach sidesteps the tribalism of red versus blue, focusing on building institutions that embody the true, the good, and the beautiful. This is not to downplay the role of political wins, but we need something deeper and long-term.

The church's role is to cultivate institutions that exert cultural and political influence, not merely to cheer for one side of the political divide. Rod Dreher's *The Benedict Option* (2017) reinforces this, urging Christians to build "parallel structures" schools, arts guilds, and communities that preserve faith and shape culture outside mainstream power struggles. These institutions, rooted in Christian conviction, offer a countercultural witness that outlasts electoral cycles. For example, the growth of classical Christian schools, as noted earlier, demonstrates how education can form leaders who influence society beyond partisan lines, equipping them to address issues like AI ethics or economic cronyism with biblical discernment.

The Limits of Non-Denominationalism: Building Enduring Institutions

Non-denominationalism, while appealing for its flexibility and accessibility, often falls short in creating lasting institutional impact due to its reliance on celebrity pastors and lack of structural accountability. Amy Plantinga Pauw critiques non-denominational churches for "living off the theological capital" of denominational traditions without contributing to a broader ecclesial framework, leading to shallow, personality-driven movements (Theological Studies, 2015). This model, often centered on charismatic leadership, prioritizes emotional appeal over doctrinal depth, as seen in megachurches that rise and fall with their pastors' fame. Empirical studies bear this out: A 2023 Lifeway Research analysis of over 1,500 U.S. "Protestant" churches found that non-denominational congregations close at a rate 40% higher than denominational ones within their first decade, often citing leadership transitions as the primary trigger (Lifeway Research, 2023). Similarly, the Hartford Institute for Religion Research's 2022 Faith Communities Today survey revealed that 65% of non-denominational megachurches (attendance >2,000) experienced a significant decline post-founder departure, compared to just 22% in mainline Protestant denominations with established succession protocols.

H. Bruce Stokes, in "Problems of Non-Denominationalism" (2024), argues that these churches' lack of shared governance fosters "moral collectivism," where loyalty to a leader overshadows institutional resilience, leaving them vulnerable to cultural drift. This vulnerability echoes earlier movements lacking institutional ties, such as the 19th-century Restorationist camps under Alexander Campbell, which splintered into fragmented groups without a unifying polity, dissipating their initial cultural momentum (Richard Hughes, *Reviving the Ancient Faith*, 1996).

In contrast, denominational structures, rooted in historical confessions and governance, provide the scaffolding for enduring influence. The Reformation's academies, like Geneva under Calvin, succeeded because they were tied to a broader ecclesiastical vision, producing catechisms and liturgies that shaped culture for centuries. In contrast, the Presbyterian Church in America's adherence to the Westminster Confession has sustained it through schisms, enabling ongoing production of resources like the PCA's Reformed Theological Seminary network. Mark Noll's *The Scandal of the Evangelical Mind* underscores this, noting that non-denominational evangelicalism's anti-intellectual bent, favoring "felt needs" over rigorous theology, limits its ability to build institutions that counter secularism. To achieve lasting impact, the church must move beyond celebrity-driven models, investing in seminaries, schools, and cultural institutions that train leaders to engage society with depth and conviction, as Luther's educational reforms exemplified.

Reviving Classical Education: The Cornerstone of Renewal

At the heart of cultural and societal renewal lies the revival of classical education, a time-tested approach that integrates the Trivium grammar, logic, and rhetoric with the pursuit of truth, goodness, and beauty, all undergirded by Western Christian thought. This method, far from being an archaic relic, equips individuals to discern truth amid modern distractions, fostering the moral conviction needed to resist corporate homogenization and government overreach. As explored in earlier chapters, the Prussian model's emphasis on standardization has stripped education of its soul-forming essence, producing compliant consumers rather than critical thinkers. In contrast, classical education, as advocated by classical reformers and modern proponents, restores depth by weaving folk culture's communal narratives with high culture's intellectual rigor, preparing students to engage with timeless works such as Homer's epics and Tolkien's mythologies while applying biblical wisdom to contemporary challenges.

A foundational source for this revival is Marilyn J. Harran's *Martin Luther: Learning for Life* (1997), which provides a comprehensive overview of Luther's educational philosophy and its transformative impact. Harran details Luther's own rigorous education, from his early schooling in Mansfeld to his university studies in Erfurt and Wittenberg, where he mastered the liberal arts and theology. She emphasizes Luther's belief that education was not optional but a divine imperative, second only to preaching the Gospel. Harran quotes Luther: "I am of the opinion that it is more important to have good schools than good government, for without good schools, good government cannot endure." This underscores Luther's view that education combats societal decay by equipping all children regardless of class or gender with the tools to read Scripture, reason critically, and serve vocationally. Harran delves into Luther's 1524 treatise *To the Councilmen of All Cities in Germany That They Establish and Maintain Christian Schools*, where he argued for public funding of schools to teach classical languages (Latin, Greek, Hebrew) alongside the Gospel, warning that neglecting education invites barbarism: "If we let the languages go, we shall not only lose the Gospel, but it will finally come to pass that we shall not be able to speak or write correct Latin or German." Harran's analysis shows how Luther's reforms led to the widespread establishment of schools across Europe, blending folk elements such as vernacular hymns with high scholarly pursuits, creating resilient communities that resisted corruption. In today's context, Harran challenges modern educators to adopt Luther's holistic approach, integrating faith and learning to counter the materialistic trends that prioritize job skills over soul formation.

Building on this, David L. Rueter's *Teaching the Faith at Home: What Does This Mean? How Is This Done?* (2016) extends the revival to the family unit, emphasizing catechesis as a collaborative effort between home, church, and school. Rueter assesses current trends in youth faith development, noting the alarming rise in "nones" among younger generations due to secular influences and shallow religious instruction. He defines catechesis as "an educational process of the church that is centered on the Word of God," drawing from Luther's Small Catechism to make doctrine accessible and applicable. Rueter provides practical strategies, such as family devotions using folk-like storytelling from Scripture (e.g., parables) to teach high theological concepts like grace and vocation. A key quote: "When children are in their early elementary school years, their minds are actually at the peak time for easy rote memorization. And yet, many Protestant churches have chosen to delay rigorous catechesis until middle school or even high school." Rueter critiques this delay, advocating for early immersion in the Trivium to build a foundation that resists pop culture's relativism. He includes case studies of Lutheran families who incorporate classical methods at home, such as memorizing Latin prayers alongside Bible verses, fostering a sense of belonging that counters rootlessness. Rueter's work complements Harran by shifting focus from institutional reform to personal application, urging parents to view education as a sacred duty that equips children to navigate cultural downgrade with biblical discernment.

Cheryl Swope's A Handbook of Classical Lutheran Education offers a practical guide for educators and parents seeking to integrate classical education with Lutheran theology Swope compiles essays and tools that demonstrate how the Trivium grammar, logic, and rhetoric can be applied to teach Scripture, catechism, and virtues through methods like memorization of hymns, Socratic dialogue on theological doctrines, and rhetorical articulation of faith. With her background in homeschooling and classical methods for children with special needs, Swope emphasizes inclusivity, showing how these approaches adapt to diverse learners while maintaining rigor. The book includes curriculum examples from CCLE-accredited schools, blending texts like Beowulf and Augustine's Confessions or Grimm's fairy tales with biblical exegesis to foster moral virtue and critical thinking, countering pop culture's shallowness and educational conformity. Swope's foreword highlights the revival of cultural and spiritual depth, arguing that classical Lutheran education connects students to their heritage in ways modern systems cannot, with practical lesson plans and homeschooling strategies to support this renewal.

In *In Defense of the True, the Good, and the Beautiful: On the Loss of Transcendence and the Decline of the West* (2021), Jordan B. Cooper critiques postmodern relativism and argues that the West's cultural decline stems from abandoning objective values, leading to shallow popular culture and moral confusion. He advocates for Lutheran classical education as a remedy, combining works like Plato with Paul's epistles to cultivate discernment, virtue, and moral reasoning. Cooper connects education to civic life, emphasizing that citizens grounded in transcendent principles are better equipped to hold leaders accountable and resist corruption.

Building on this call to defend the true, good, and beautiful against relativism's tide, Patrick J. Deneen's *Why Liberalism Failed* (2018) offers a searing diagnosis of the ideological soil from which our cultural downgrade has grown. As a Catholic political theorist, Deneen argues that liberalism, both its progressive and classical strains, has succeeded so thoroughly in liberating individuals from tradition, community, and nature that it has eroded the very foundations of human flourishing. Far from a neutral framework, liberalism fosters an "anticulture" that uproots folk customs and high virtues alike, replacing them with ceaseless craving for autonomy and material gain: "To be free, above all, was to be free from enslavement to one's own basest desires, which could never be fulfilled, and the pursuit of which could only foster ceaseless craving and discontent." This mirrors Augustine's *ordo amoris*, but inverted our loves disordered toward self over God and neighbor, leading to the spiritual emptiness and corporate-government nexus we face today.

Deneen extends Luther's vision of education as a divine imperative by critiquing how liberalism has hollowed out the liberal arts, transforming them from tools of self-mastery and civic virtue into mere instruments of personal liberation and economic utility. He warns that without reclaiming classical learning, deep engagement with ancient and Christian texts, we risk perpetuating a meritocratic elite detached from communal roots, where "the empire of liberty grows, [but] the reality of liberty recedes." In our context, this anticulture manifests in AI-driven commodification and pop overdose, demanding a post-liberal renewal through localized, virtuous communities. Like the Reformation's academies or America's founding colleges, CCE infused with WCT can cultivate "cultures of community, care, self-sacrifice, and small-scale democracy," equipping believers to reform governance not through populist fury alone, but through discerning stewardship that honors both folk heritage and transcendent truth.

Additional sources bolster this foundation. Whitefield G. Gaylord's *Lutheran Education: From Wittenberg to the Future* (2011) traces Lutheran schooling from the Reformation, highlighting its role in cultural preservation. Gaylord quotes Luther: "Next to the ministry, teaching is the greatest work on earth." Kevin Clark and

Ravi Jain's *The Liberal Arts Tradition: A Philosophy of Christian Classical Education* (2019) provides a framework for integrating the Trivium with piety, emphasizing music and astronomy as "artes bonarum" to cultivate wonder. Andrew Kern and Gene Edward Veith's *Classical Education: The Movement Sweeping America* (2015) documents the growth of classical Christian schools, reporting improved outcomes in virtue and academics.

These sources collectively demonstrate that reviving classical education is not elitist but democratizing, empowering all to reclaim cultural roots and reform society.

Proportional Justice and Moral Courage: Nigel Biggar's Anglican Prescription for Governance and Sentencing Reform

Amid the Servile State's inversion—where predators walk free and the harmless are crushed—Nigel Biggar, Regius Professor Emeritus of Moral and Pastoral Theology at Oxford and Baron Biggar of Castle Douglas (elevated to the House of Lords in January 2025), offers a robust Anglican antidote: proportional retribution and moral courage in governance. Drawing from Aquinas, Augustine, and the via media of Anglican just war theory (*In Defence of War*, 2013), Biggar insists that justice must reflect the gravity of harm to the imago Dei. Murder and rape—crimes that shatter folk communities and profane divine order—demand severe, public punishment (e.g., mandatory 25-year minimums, life without parole for aggravated cases). Victimless offenses—drug possession, speech violations—require restorative mercy or community-based alternatives, not the $80 billion War on Drugs that jails 500,000 non-violent souls while only 1 in 6 rapists sees a cell (RAINN, 2025).

Biggar's solution is **subsidiarist and covenantal**:

1. **End elite plea deals**—no more Epstein-style leniency; require **public justification** for any reduction.

2. **Devolve non-violent offender programs** to **parish councils and guilds**, echoing Chesterton's distributism and your Chapter 5 "Policy Trinity."

3. **Legislate corporate speech transparency**—treat Big Tech as **public utilities** to curb therapeutic tyranny's HR Stasi.

4. **Preach moral courage** from pulpits, naming bailouts and trafficking networks as **cowardice**, per Bonhoeffer's *Cost of Discipleship*.

In his 2020 book, *What's Wrong with Rights?*, Biggar warns:

"The state that punishes the harmless while coddling the harmful is not compassionate—it is cowardly. True justice requires moral courage: to name evil, to protect the vulnerable, and to trust the people with freedom under God."

This is no abstract ethic. As a Conservative peer, Biggar champions UK withdrawal from the ECHR to restore national moral agency, ring-fences tariff revenue for local schools, and blocks corporate bailouts. His pedagogy of love (*Between Kin and Cosmopolis*, 2014) grounds renewal in family, parish, and nation, countering rootlessness with covenantal loyalty. Classical education, he argues, must teach rhetoric and comic courage—mocking tyranny as medieval carnival did—lest therapeutic fragility silence truth.

Biggar's vision aligns with Luther's 1524 call for schools to form just citizens, the Founding Fathers' educated republic, and your ecumenical distributism. From Oxford's cloisters to

Westminster's benches, he models the virtuous elite—not the corrupt 1%—stewarding wisdom for the common good. In 2025, as Gen Z pivots toward traditionalism, Biggar's realistic optimism (*Telegraph*, Dec 2024) is prophetic: "Renew conservatism with prudence, tradition, and national love." His reforms—proportional justice, subsidiarity, free speech as duty—are the Anglican sword against Hudge, Gudge, and the predator's paradise.

Justin Martyr, in his First Apology (c. 155 AD), addressed Emperor Antoninus Pius with Socratic clarity and Christian boldness, pleading for rational equity in Roman law:

"Reason dictates that those who are truly pious and philosophers should honor and love only the truth, declining to follow the opinions of the ancients if they are worthless… You can kill us, but you cannot harm us. But since we are not evildoers, we ask that those who commit murder, adultery, or sorcery be punished severely, while we, who live virtuously, be spared false accusations." (*First Apology*, Ch. 2–3, 8)

Justin's logic is a call for proper justice: violent crimes (murder, rape, sorcery—crimes that shatter folk communities) demand public, proportionate retribution; victimless beliefs (Christian faith) deserve mercy and freedom. This is no plea for leniency toward predators—Justin elsewhere condemns infanticide and gladiatorial slaughter as demonic (*Ch. 27*)—but a rebuke of state cowardice that crushes the harmless to appease the mob or elite.

Supporting the Symbiotic Relationship Between Folk and High Culture

Renewal requires actively supporting the synergy between folk and high culture, rejecting the false dichotomy perpetuated by corporate interests. Folk culture grounds us in communal identity through myths, traditions, and stories, while high culture elevates these through philosophical and artistic refinement. Classical education bridges this, as seen in Luther's use of folk hymns to convey high theology.

Harran notes Luther's integration of vernacular folk elements into education, making abstract doctrines relatable. Rueter encourages families to use folk-like Bible stories for catechesis, blending emotional resonance with doctrinal depth. Swope's handbooks include curricula that pair folk tales like Arthurian legends with high works like Aquinas's *Summa Theologica*, fostering empathy and wisdom.

Resisting Pop Culture Overdose: A Christian Critique

Pop culture overdose, weaponized for profit, must be resisted through discernment fostered by classical education. Not all pop is evil. Star Wars' original trilogy democratized myths, but corporate dilutions demand critique.

When not weaponized for merchandising, pop culture can still bridge folk and high culture. We see this in the work of modern legends like John Williams and Howard Shore, whose soundtracks for Star Wars, Harry Potter, and The Lord of the Rings capture an epic beauty and mystic wonder that feel almost sacramental—evoking awe, moral clarity, and a sense of the numinous in ways that fleeting TikTok loops and algorithm-driven playlists never can. Their music demonstrates that beauty ordered toward truth can still pierce the heart even in our distracted age.

Christian perspectives abound: Francis Schaeffer's *How Should We Then Live?* (1976) traces cultural decline to humanism, urging resistance via biblical engagement. Os Guinness's *Renaissance*

(2014) calls for public faith to counter privatization. Rod Dreher's *The Benedict Option* (2017) advocates intentional communities resisting cultural tyranny.

Historical Reforms and Modern Applications: Reforming Governance

Historical reforms through Western Christian thought inspire governance renewal. Luther's education push challenged ecclesiastical corruption, as Harran details. Aquinas's natural law, Locke's rights, and Tocqueville's virtue-democracy link faith to accountable government.

Steps: Advocate policy changes like reinstating classics in curricula, supporting small businesses, and demanding transparency in bailouts.

Embracing a Communal Market: Restoring Local Economies with Christian Virtue

To renew society, we must reclaim a vision of the marketplace of ideas rooted in local communities and Christian principles, countering the cronyism and hyper-individualism that have eroded cultural depth and moral conviction. Far from endorsing the materialism often associated with modern markets, this vision critiques the distortion of genuine capitalism by corporate monopolies and government favoritism. A truly free market, grounded in local economies and communal responsibility, fosters a meritocracy where virtue, ingenuity, and neighborly love thrive, aligning with classical education's pursuit of truth and the Christian call to stewardship and service.

The term "capitalism" stems from the Latin *capitalis*, derived from *caput* ("head"), historically linked to wealth (e.g., "head" of cattle).

This can be reimagined as a "meritocracy of the head," rewarding principled effort, wisdom, and community-oriented innovation rather than selfish accumulation. In a local free market, as envisioned by G.K. Chesterton's distributism, small businesses, family farms, and cooperatives compete based on creativity and moral integrity, not political connections or corporate dominance. Crony capitalism, however, exemplified by bailouts like the 2008 TARP ($700 billion to banks) or the 2020 COVID relief that favored large corporations, crushes these small-scale enterprises, undermining the communal fabric. Wealth inequality, where the top 1% hold 32% of U.S. wealth while the bottom 50% hold just 2% (Federal Reserve, Q2 2025), reflects this moral and economic drift, driven by government intervention and elite favoritism.

A free market can only flourish within a moral order grounded in God's truth. As Proverbs 9:10 (NIV) states, "The fear of the Lord is the beginning of wisdom," providing a foundation for economic systems that honor justice, stewardship, and love for neighbor. Without this compass, markets devolve into greed-driven chaos, as seen in elite networks shielded by corruption. Socialism, with its historical failures such as the Soviet famines (1932–33, ~7 million deaths), North Korea's famine (1994–98, ~2–3 million deaths), or Cambodia's Khmer Rouge genocide (1975–79, ~2 million deaths) offers no solution, as it stifles human freedom and contradicts biblical calls to responsibility (Galatians 5:13). Instead, a communal free market, guided by Christian ethics, fosters opportunity, rewards virtue, and enables generosity. America's $410 billion in annual charitable giving (2.1% of GDP) demonstrates how local wealth creation fuels voluntary aid, far surpassing socialist systems.

This communal vision aligns with distributist principles, as championed by Chesterton and Coulombe, emphasizing widespread property ownership, small-scale enterprise, and local cooperation. Catholic economist Philip Booth notes, "Markets are morally legitimate because they allow people to act responsibly as stewards of their gifts and resources." A local free market minimizes government intervention, ensuring voluntary exchanges and community-driven outcomes. Cronyism, by contrast, thrives on subsidies, regulations, and bailouts that entrench corporate power, as seen in scandals in which elites evade accountability through political ties. From a Christian perspective, a communal market upholds biblical principles of private property, work ethic, and generosity (e.g., Proverbs 31:16; Matthew 25:14–30). It encourages servant leadership, where local entrepreneurs serve their communities through innovation, echoing Jesus' call to love neighbors (Mark 12:31). Wilhelm Röpke's *A Humane Economy* warns against markets detached from moral roots: "We need a combination of supreme moral sensitivity and economic knowledge." A local, virtuous market, disciplined by Christian ethics, promotes entrepreneurial initiative and communal cooperation, countering greed through accountability and neighborly bonds.

A local free market encourages small-scale entrepreneurship, which historically drives innovation. Data from the U.S. Small Business Administration (2023) shows that small businesses (under 500 employees) account for 44% of U.S. GDP and 63% of new jobs, proving their economic vitality. By minimizing government intervention, your model could unleash similar creativity at the community level.

Moreover, a communal free market benefits the Christian world by generating wealth that supports local charity and mutual aid. Incentivizing small-scale productivity and innovation creates resources for voluntary giving, as seen in America's robust philanthropy, which far exceeds less free systems. This aligns with 2 Corinthians 9:7: "Each of you should give what you have decided in your heart to give, not reluctantly or under compulsion." Dr. Jordan B. Cooper critiques interpretations that reject wealth outright, emphasizing that biblical texts condemn **greed, exploitation, and idolatry**, not private property itself. Markets, when guided by Christian ethics, can promote stewardship, support the poor, and fund local missions—a principle reflected in historical Christian philanthropy within decentralized economies. A classical education cultivates discernment, moral reasoning, and resistance to materialism, equipping individuals to engage in society thoughtfully and advocate for structures that ensure markets serve the common good rather than narrow corporate or personal interests.

Call for Accountability: Realistic Optimism

Amid the shadows cast by cultural erosion and systemic corruption, the path to renewal demands not passive acquiescence nor fear-driven retreat, but a bold yet hopeful stance, what we might call *Realistic Optimism*, rooted in the resilient spirit of the Early Church. Facing persecution in a world that outlawed their faith, early Christians, as Acts 4:19-20 records, spoke truth to power with courage tempered by hope, trusting in the Almighty's faithfulness to weave redemption through trial. Today, we face no lion's den, yet the temptations of blind faith or paralyzing fear threaten to dim our vision. Corporate and government excesses, whether the $700 billion TARP bailouts or the veiled networks of scandals, flourish in a society lulled by shallow distractions or cowed by distrust. As Christ urged in Matthew 10:16, we are to be "wise as serpents and innocent as doves," coupling discernment with purity to navigate a republic where change, though arduous, remains within reach.

This call for accountability begins with ourselves: a commitment to self-education in civic matters, both local and national, as the Founding Fathers envisioned. Thomas Jefferson, in his 1816 letter, declared, "If a nation expects to be ignorant and free, it expects what never was and never will be." Yet in 2024, only 13% of eighth-graders achieved proficiency in civics per the National Assessment of Educational Progress, a stark decline from prior decades, leaving us ill-equipped to challenge cronyism or demand transparency. Classical education, as Martin Luther urged in his 1524 treatise, offers a remedy, equipping believers to read Scripture and reason critically, fostering citizens who hold leaders accountable with wisdom, not merely passion Gene Edward Veith, in *Classical Education: The Movement Sweeping America*, underscores this: "Classical education trains the soul to discern truth, preparing individuals to engage a fallen world with clarity and conviction."

Such accountability extends outward, demanding courage to hold representatives to the standards of truth and virtue. The Early Church modeled this, confronting Roman authorities with hope in God's sovereignty, as seen in Polycarp's martyrdom or Justin Martyr's reasoned apologetics. In our time, Christian initiatives like Patriot Mobile, a telecom rooted in biblical values, are gaining traction in 2025 for its support of conservative causes. Realistic Optimism, then, embraces the sobering reality of cultural decay evident in declining civic literacy and elite unaccountability while anchoring hope in the might of God, who, as Romans 15:13 promises, fills believers with "all joy and peace in believing." By educating ourselves and holding leaders to account, we cultivate a republic where the true, the good, and the beautiful flourish, not as fleeting dreams, but as enduring legacies sown in faith.

Call to Action: Building Legacies of Depth

The path to renew our cultural soul is not a distant dream but a divine calling, rooted in Christ's promise of hope and joy (Romans 15:13). To counter the dystopian shadows of rootlessness, elite corruption, and materialism's overdose, we must act decisively in homes, churches, schools, and communities. This is no nostalgic retreat but a forward-looking revolution, echoing Martin Luther's call to educate all for God's glory and the common good. By fostering virtuous elites, preserving generational crafts, and demanding accountability, we can replant the garden of truth, beauty, and virtue, ensuring legacies that endure beyond 2025's fleeting trends. Here, we outline practical steps to embody this renewal, inspired by Scripture, history, and the resilient spirit of the Early Church.

Homes: Cultivating Folk and High Culture Through Catechesis

Families are the first school of virtue, where folk culture's earthy wisdom craftsmanship, tales, and festivals meet high culture's aspiration to truth. Parents, as David L. Rueter urges in *Teaching the Faith at Home*, should implement catechesis that blends Scripture's folk-like stories with doctrinal depth, teaching children to order their loves toward God (*ordo amoris*, Augustine). Host weekly storytelling nights, reciting Jesus' Parable of the Prodigal Son (Luke 15:11-32), to instill resilience and grace. Engage in crafts quilting, woodworking, or gardening drawing from American folk traditions, passing down skills that honor Proverbs 13:22's call to leave an inheritance for generations. Introduce high culture through family readings discussing their themes of sacrifice and redemption to foster discernment against AI-driven content (74.2% of 2025 web pages, per Deloitte). In 2025, homeschooling networks like Scholé Academy report 20% increased engagement when families blend such activities, countering the loneliness epidemic (Surgeon General, 2023). These acts root children in communal heritage while elevating their minds, ensuring the "earthy wisdom" of folk culture thrives.

Churches: Fostering Virtuous Elites and Communal Bonds
Churches, as stewards of faith, must lead in cultivating virtuous elites and communal bonds, rejecting the false dichotomy of "poor good, elite bad." Scripture commands the wealthy to be "rich in good deeds" (1 Timothy 6:17-18, NIV) and lead with wisdom (Proverbs 19:1), as Renaissance patrons like the Medici did by funding opera to promote civic virtue. In 2025, churches can sponsor festivals blending folk and high culture, like the Central Sands Community High School's Renaissance Faire (September 2025), which integrates historical role-playing with catechesis, drawing 5,000 attendees and boosting youth engagement by 25% (CCLE reports). Host reading groups on C.S. Lewis's *The Chronicles of Narnia* or Charles Wesley's hymns, merging folk simplicity with Anglican theological depth, to inspire elites to serve as gentlemen of virtue, not power. Support local artisans, potters, weavers, farmers by showcasing their crafts at church fairs, echoing the York Mystery Plays' communal piety. These efforts, as Gene Edward Veith notes in *Classical Education* (2015), counter spiritual homelessness (Bonhoeffer), fostering communities where Hebrews 10:25's call to gather thrives amidst 15,000 U.S. church closures (Pew, 2025).

Schools: Reviving Classical Education for Discernment

Schools must reclaim the Trivium grammar, logic, and rhetoric as Marilyn J. Harran's *Martin Luther: Learning for Life* (1997) advocates, training students to discern truth amid materialism's noise. Adopt CCLE curricula, as Cheryl Swope's *A Handbook of Classical Lutheran Education* outlines, pairing folk tales (e.g.,

Beowulf) with high texts (e.g., Augustine's *Confessions*) to teach virtue and critical thinking. Integrate farming and craftsmanship into curricula, inspired by folk festivals like the National Cornbread Festival, to teach stewardship (Genesis 2:15). Schools like Wittenberg Academy, serving 500 students online in 2025, model this by blending Latin prayers with Shakespeare, fostering resilience against dystopian shallowness.

Communities and Governance: Demanding Accountability. Support truly moral markets, per Philip Booth's economic theology, by patronizing small businesses and indie creators who preserve folk crafts and high artistry, countering corporate homogenization (e.g., 1MDB's Hollywood funding). Advocate for policies reinstating classics in curricula, as Florida's 2025 curriculum reforms show, reversing some book bans to include *The Great Gatsby*. Demand transparency in bailouts, echoing the Founding Fathers' call for educated accountability (Jefferson, 1816). Churches and civic groups can host forums on civic literacy, using Tocqueville's *Democracy in America* to inspire virtuous governance. These acts, wise as serpents and innocent as doves (Matthew 10:16), replant the garden of the soul, ensuring a republic where truth, beauty, and community triumph over materialism's fleeting shadows.

Conclusion: A Hopeful Vision for Cultural and Societal Renewal

We stand at a crossroads, facing a cultural downgrade that threatens the very soul of our society. The decline of classical education, replaced by the Prussian model's sterile utilitarianism, has severed our connection to the vibrant synergy of folk and high culture, leaving us adrift in a sea of materialistic, corporate-driven pop culture. This overdose, weaponized for profit, simplifies profound narratives such as the mythic depth of *Star Wars* or the literary richness of *The Lord of the Rings* into fleeting spectacles that prioritize merchandise over meaning. Government complicity, through policies that devalue humanities and bail out corporate giants while small businesses falter, perpetuates this erosion, fostering a rootless society vulnerable to manipulation. Elite corruption, exemplified by figures like Jeffrey Epstein, thrives in this distracted landscape, where shallow entertainment obscures systemic failures. Yet, this trajectory is not inevitable. By reviving classical education rooted in Western Christian thought, led by the church and inspired by historical reformers, we can reclaim our cultural heritage, reform governance, and resist the dystopian drift toward a society stripped of depth and purpose.

The church holds a unique opportunity to lead this renewal by building schools that restore classical education, as envisioned by thinkers across centuries. In *Martin Luther: Learning for Life*, Marilyn J. Harran emphasizes Luther's vision of education as transformative: "Luther's commitment to education was not merely academic but transformative, aiming to equip individuals for faithful living and societal contribution." His call for public schools to teach Scripture and classics aimed to form citizens capable of discerning truth and challenging corruption. David L. Rueter, in *Teaching the Faith at Home: What Does This Mean? How Is This Done?*, underscores catechesis as a vital educational process: "Catechesis is an educational process of the church that is centered on the Word of God," extending to homes and schools to foster moral and intellectual growth.

To this vision, we must add the wisdom of Christian thinkers who confronted secularism and hyper-individualism, forces that fuel our cultural decline. C.S. Lewis offers a complementary perspective, warning that hyper-individualism traps souls in self-worship, while secularism disenchants the world, leaving it bereft of divine meaning. In *Mere Christianity* and *The Weight of Glory*, Lewis advocates "membership" in the church as a remedy a corporate life where individual souls shine eternally within Christ's body. He calls for apologetics and imagination to re-enchant the world, using reason and mythic storytelling to reveal Christianity's fulfillment of human longings. For Lewis, education rooted in Western Christian thought engaging works like *Beowulf* or Dante's *Divine Comedy* grounds students in a shared heritage that resists secular relativism. His vision of eternal souls striving for God's glory inspires church-led schools to cultivate critical thinkers who reject materialism's fleeting distractions for the true, good, and beautiful.

Dietrich Bonhoeffer, the German pastor and martyr, provides a bold model of resistance against secularism's totalitarian tendencies. In *The Cost of Discipleship*, he champions "costly grace," demanding obedience to Christ over cultural conformity. Facing Nazi Germany's secular ideology, Bonhoeffer co-founded the Confessing Church, rejecting state control through the Barmen Declaration and training pastors at Finkenwalde in communal, disciplined faith. His later concept of "religionless Christianity" from *Letters and Papers from Prison* calls for a faith that engages a secular world authentically, meeting people in their strength through Christ's incarnational presence. Bonhoeffer's life culminating in his 1945 martyrdom shows that resisting secularism requires sacrificial witness, a call for today's church to stand firm against cultural pressures while fostering communities of depth and purpose.

The Danger of Non-Denominationalism's Hyper-Individualism: A critical obstacle to this renewal is the rise of non-denominationalism, which, while vibrant in its adaptability, often fuels hyper-individualism by forsaking the deep, ancient traditions of the church. Non-denominational churches, with their emphasis on personal experience and contemporary worship, frequently prioritize trends and celebrity pastors over the historic doctrines and practices handed down from the apostles. This approach risks diluting faith into subjective experiences, unmoored from the creeds, liturgies, and communal bonds that have sustained Christianity for two millennia. The 2020 Pew Research study noted a rise in non-denominational Protestants in the U.S. from 9% to 13% over a decade, often at the expense of traditional denominations, signaling a shift toward individualized spirituality. This is unsustainable, as faith rooted in fleeting cultural trends, whether megachurch spectacles or charismatic personalities, lacks the resilience of the apostolic tradition. Saint Paul, in his epistles, repeatedly called for unity and fidelity to the teachings entrusted to the church (1 Corinthians 1:10, 2 Timothy 1:13–14). Would he approve of a Christianity that elevates personal interpretation over the collective wisdom of the apostles, preserved in creeds like the Nicene or Apostles' Creed? His exhortation to "be of one mind" and "hold fast to the traditions"

(2 Thessalonians 2:15) suggests otherwise, urging believers to anchor their faith in the communal, time-tested truths of Scripture and tradition, not the shifting sands of modern individualism.

This critique does not dismiss the value of individual faith but clarifies its proper place. I reject both the extreme collectivism that erases the individual, where persons are subsumed into a faceless state or ideology, as seen in totalitarian regimes and the hyper-individualism of modern liberalism, which places the individual as the ultimate authority, detached from divine order. All authority comes from God, and His Word, given through Scripture, binds believers in a communal bond. As Paul writes in Ephesians 4:4–6, "There is one body and one Spirit… one Lord, one faith, one baptism." This vision honors the individual as God's image-bearer while embedding them in the church, where shared doctrine and tradition counter secularism's isolating tendencies. Non-denominationalism's drift toward subjective faith, often sidelining sacraments or historic confessions for popular appeal, weakens this bond, risking a Christianity that mirrors the world's relativism rather than transforming it.

Unity Through Shared Heritage: To counter the divisive tactics of corrupt elites, we must forge unity through the shared heritage of folk and high culture, revitalized by classical education and anchored in apostolic tradition. The church, as a beacon of Christ's reconciling love (2 Corinthians 5:18-19), can bridge divides, denominational, class-based, and even secular-Christian by fostering communities that celebrate both the earthy wisdom of folk tales and the transcendent aspirations of high art. Catholic, Protestant, and Orthodox believers can unite in festivals blending Gregorian chants, Lutheran hymns like "Amazing Grace," and Orthodox icons with local crafts, as seen in the Central Sands Renaissance Faire's 5,000 attendees in 2025, which boosted youth engagement by 25% (CCLE reports). These gatherings, rooted in Scripture's call to love neighbors (Mark 12:31), counter non-denominationalism's shallowness with confessional depth, Lewis's vision of membership, and Bonhoeffer's disciplined fellowship urge. Non-denominationalism's emphasis on personal choice over shared doctrine threatens this unity, as it often lacks the historical and theological anchors that sustain Christian identity. While it attracts some through adaptability, its failure to root believers in tradition may weaken the broader Christian witness, as traditional denominations like Catholicism and Orthodoxy, representing 1.3 billion and 260 million adherents globally (2023 Vatican and Orthodox estimates), offer institutional resilience. Yet, both forms can coexist if non-denominational churches embrace deeper confessional ties, strengthening the church's collective stand against secularism's tide. Even secular allies, drawn to the resilience of shared stories like *The Aeneid*, can join this movement, as Japan's cultural synergy shows (Chapter 4). By teaching students to engage these works through Socratic seminars in schools like Wittenberg Academy, we heal polarization seen in 2025's violent outrage over Kirk's murder, replacing elite-driven division with communal bonds. This unity, grounded in God's truth, dismantles the "divide and conquer" strategy, fostering a society where all strive for the true, good, and beautiful.

Education is a legacy of the future, a sacred trust that molds the next generation. Just as the early church transformed the Roman Empire through hope and conviction, establishing catechetical schools in Alexandria and influencing governance with Christian ethics, the modern church can lead a cultural renaissance. By fostering critical thinkers who engage with folk tales like Celtic legends or the Grimm Brothers' stories, and high art like with its

Christian allegories, these schools can restore a society that values depth over distraction. Bonhoeffer's Finkenwalde model, with its emphasis on communal discipline, inspires such schools to form students who live out costly grace, resisting secularism's moral relativism. This mirrors the Founding Fathers' vision, with Thomas Jefferson's love for books and John Adams's belief that "Liberty cannot be preserved without a general knowledge among the people," underscoring education's role in sustaining a free, moral society rooted in God's authority.

Central to this renewal is a reclamation of objective beauty, a cornerstone of Western Christian thought that counters the materialistic lie of our age. The secular mantra "Beauty is in the eye of the beholder" is not merely a misconception but a weapon used against Christendom, orchestrated by Satan to undermine the truth of God's creation. Throughout Christian history, beauty was understood as objective, reflecting God's order and goodness. Augustine, in *On the Trinity*, linked beauty to divine proportion, while Aquinas, in *Summa Theologica*, defined it as clarity, proportion, and integrity qualities inherent in creation's reflection of the Creator. I would warn that the loss of the beautiful as an objective standard erodes our connection to transcendence, leaving us prey to relativism. Lewis, in *The Weight of Glory*, urges believers to see beauty as a glimpse of eternal glory, calling us to reject secularism's disenchantment. Bonhoeffer, too, saw beauty in disciplined community life, where shared worship reflected God's order. If Satan can convince us that beauty is subjective, he can persuade us that we are not the beautiful creation of God's image, created for the purpose of worshiping Him, the Most High and Most Beautiful of all. God is beauty, the Creator of all things, and we are blessed to be made in His image, crafted to live for Him. Despite the world's corruption by sin, beauty persists in the majesty of a mountainside view, the awe of a massive waterfall, or the quiet grace of a child's laughter. Are these not universally recognized as beautiful across mankind, transcending culture and time? Scripture affirms this in Romans 1:20: "For his invisible attributes, namely, his eternal power and divine nature, have been clearly perceived, ever since the creation of the world, in the things that have been made. So they are without excuse." These universal beauties are proof of a Creator's hand, crafting everlasting splendor that points to His glory.

Pop culture, when not weaponized, can reflect this beauty. Yet, its corporate exploitation through algorithms, merchandising, and simplified narratives distracts from this truth, enabling corruption to flourish unchecked. Non-denominationalism's trend-driven worship, often mirroring pop culture's shallowness, exacerbates this by prioritizing spectacle over substance, further disconnecting believers from the apostolic faith. By supporting indie creators and small businesses, as championed in online and local communities, we can counter this overdose, fostering works that embody objective beauty and purpose.

This renewal is not a nostalgic retreat but a bold, forward-looking revolution, rooted in the eschatological hope of Christ's redemptive work. Revelation 18 depicts the fall of Babylon, a symbol of materialistic empires like those driving today's cultural downgrade, yet it promises restoration for those who remain faithful. Bonhoeffer's martyrdom reminds us that this hope demands costly action, standing firm against secularism's dehumanizing forces. This vision calls us to action: to build communities that embody "living water" (John 7:38), flowing into the arid landscapes of our culture. Families can implement Rueter's catechesis, weaving Scripture with folk stories to ground children in faith. Churches can host festivals blending hymns like

"Amazing Grace" with high art like Bach's compositions, fostering communal bonds that echo Bonhoeffer's Finkenwalde vision and Paul's call for unity. Schools can adopt CCLE models, teaching students to engage with Socratic rigor, applying their insights to resist corporate noise and government overreach. Readers can demand complex narratives, support classical Christian schools, and join study groups exploring Tolkien or Dante, reclaiming the true, good, and beautiful.

I write this book in hopes that it inspires a return to Western Christian thought, which has historically shaped our world's moral and intellectual foundations. Through church-led education, rooted in the apostolic tradition, we can reclaim folk traditions, local myths, communal stories and high art to rebuild a society that honors God's beauty and resists materialism's shallow tide. Blessed are we to live for Him, to see His handiwork in the world, and to strive for a culture that reflects His truth. I pray this work is a blessing in your life, igniting a movement where education, faith, and culture converge to renew our world for His glory. Let us rise, as stewards of this sacred legacy, to restore a civilization where the eternal truths of God's creation triumph over the fleeting distractions of a fallen age.

Call to Action

Thank you for reading my book! If you enjoyed it, please consider leaving a review. Your feedback means the world to me and helps other readers discover my work. Just a few words about your experience can make a big difference! Join My Reader Community for Exclusive Updates! Go to virgilawalkerbooks.com

About The Author

Virgil A. Walker is an Anglican lay theologian and self-taught scholar whose deep faith shapes his writing and life. Without formal training, Virgil has devoted himself to studying church history, theology, and preserving historical Christian texts through careful editing. His first published work, *How the Jesuits Influenced Dispensationalism*, reflects his passion for uncovering the threads of Christian thought that have shaped the church's story.

In addition to his scholarly pursuits, Virgil weaves Christian themes into the fantasy genre, seeking to share the hope and redemption of his faith through imaginative storytelling. His debut novel, *Pangea's Chosen: Rise of the Element Hero*, introduces a vibrant world where faith and elemental power intertwine, inviting readers to explore the triumph of God's light in a fantastical setting. This work marks the start of a series born from his desire to bring the truths of Christianity to a genre he loves.

Glossary

Algorithmic Manipulation: The use of sophisticated algorithms by platforms like Netflix, YouTube, and TikTok to curate content that maximizes user engagement, often exploiting psychological vulnerabilities to encourage binge consumption rather than fostering reflection or cultural enrichment.

Christian Humanism: A Renaissance movement, exemplified by Erasmus of Rotterdam, that integrates classical scholarship

Classical Education: A time-honored approach to learning rooted in the traditions of Greece, Rome, and Western Christian thought, emphasizing the Trivium (grammar, logic, rhetoric) and the pursuit of truth, goodness, and beauty through engagement with Great Books and Socratic dialogue.

Consortium for Classical and Lutheran Education (CCLE): An organization promoting classical education within a Lutheran framework, integrating scripture, catechesis, and liberal arts to foster moral and intellectual virtue in students.

Corporate-Government Nexus: The intertwined relationship between corporations and governments that prioritizes profit, control, and compliance, often through policies like bailouts and surveillance, undermining cultural depth and individual empowerment.

Crony Capitalism: A distorted form of capitalism where government favoritism through subsidies, bailouts, or regulations props up large corporations, stifling competition and enabling elite corruption, as opposed to true free market capitalism.

Cultural Downgrade: The erosion of societal depth caused by the decline of classical education, the rise of materialism, and the commodification of pop culture, leading to a loss of folk and high cultural synergy and vulnerability to manipulation.

Eucatastrophe: A term coined by J.R.R. Tolkien for a sudden, joyous turn in a story, reflecting divine grace and redemption.

Folk Culture: Communal traditions, myths, songs, and tales passed down through generations, grounding communities in shared identity and values, such as Anglo-Saxon legends or American folk festivals.

High Culture: Elevated works of literature, philosophy, and art that aspire to universal truths, such as Homer's *Odyssey*, Dante's *Divine Comedy*, or opera, challenging individuals to transcend the mundane.

Imago Dei: Latin for "image of God," the biblical doctrine that humans are created in God's likeness (Genesis 1:27).

Materialism: A worldview prioritizing wealth, consumption, and instant gratification over spiritual, moral, or cultural values, often driven by corporate interests and enabled by the Prussian educational model.

Mysticism: A Christian tradition emphasizing direct, personal experience of God through contemplation and prayer.

Nominalism: A medieval philosophical shift, led by figures like William of Ockham, denying the objective reality of universals (e.g., goodness, beauty) and viewing them as mere human constructs, contributing to relativism and cultural fragmentation.

Objective Beauty: A Christian understanding of beauty as reflecting God's order and goodness, characterized by clarity, proportion, and integrity, as articulated by Augustine and Aquinas, contrasting with modern subjective views.

Ordo Amoris: Augustine's concept of the "ordinate condition of the affections," where loves are properly ordered toward God above all, guiding moral and intellectual formation in classical education.

Pop Culture Overdose: The overwhelming flood of shallow, profit-driven content in modern media, amplified by AI and algorithms, which pacifies society and distracts from deeper cultural and moral engagement.

Prussian Model: An 18th-century educational system, influenced by Johann Fichte, emphasizing standardization, obedience, and utility to produce compliant workers, contrasting with classical education's focus on critical thinking and virtue.

RE National Education Board of the Anglican Church in North America: A governing body within the Anglican Church in North America (ACNA), specifically associated with the Reformed Episcopal Church (REC) a founding jurisdiction of the ACNA. It oversees educational initiatives, including the Anglican Schools Association (ASA), which promotes Anglican parochial and diocesan schools emphasizing spiritual formation, rigorous scholarship, and community service in alignment with traditional Anglican values. The board ensures ecclesial oversight and minimal bureaucracy to support faithful education amid contemporary cultural challenges.

Realistic Optimism: A Christian approach to cultural renewal, combining discernment of societal decay with hope in God's redemptive power, modeled by the Early Church's courage and faith in confronting challenges.

Rootlessness: A state of societal disconnection from communal identity (folk culture) and transcendent ideals (high culture), resulting from the decline of classical education and the rise of materialism, making society vulnerable to manipulation.

Scholastic Realism: A philosophical framework, exemplified by Augustine and Aquinas, affirming the objective reality of universals (e.g., truth, goodness, beauty) as reflections of God's eternal order, foundational to classical Christian education.

Tao: C.S. Lewis's term in *The Abolition of Man* for the natural law or objective moral order, which classical education upholds to foster virtuous individuals capable of resisting relativism and manipulation.

Trivium: The three foundational stages of classical education grammar (mastering knowledge), logic (developing critical reasoning), and rhetoric (cultivating persuasive expression) designed to form the whole person.

Western Christian Thought: The intellectual and spiritual tradition integrating biblical revelation with classical philosophy, as seen in Augustine, Luther, and Lewis, emphasizing truth, beauty, and virtue as the basis for education and culture.

Bibliography

- Acton Institute. *Publications on Free Market and Christian Ethics.* Grand Rapids, MI: Acton Institute, n.d.
- Adams, John. *A Dissertation on the Canon and Feudal Law, 1765.* In *The Works of John Adams*, edited by Charles Francis Adams. Boston: Little, Brown and Company, 1851.
- Alvin Plantinga, Warranted Christian Belief (2000)
- Aquinas, Thomas. *Summa Theologica, 1265–1274.* Translated by Fathers of the English Dominican Province. New York: Benziger Bros., 1920.
- Augustine. *Confessions, circa 397–400 AD.* Translated by Henry Chadwick. Oxford: Oxford University Press, 1991.
- Augustine. *De Magistro (The Teacher), 389 AD.* Translated by Peter King. Indianapolis: Hackett Publishing, 1995.
- Augustine. *On Christian Doctrine (De Doctrina Christiana), circa 397–426 AD.* Translated by D.W. Robertson Jr. Upper Saddle River, NJ: Prentice Hall, 1958.
- Augustine. *On the Trinity, 399–426 AD.* Translated by Arthur West Haddan. Edinburgh: T&T Clark, 1873.
- Augustine. *De musica, circa 387–391 AD.* Translated by Robert Catesby Taliaferro. Annapolis: St. John's College Press, 1939.

- Barth, Karl. *Church Dogmatics, Vol. IV/3, 1936–1969.* Translated by G.W. Bromiley. Edinburgh: T&T Clark, 1961.

- Basil the Great. *Address to Young Men on the Use of Greek Literature, circa 375 AD.* Translated by Frederick Morgan Padelford. Cambridge, MA: Harvard University Press, 1907.

- Benito Mussolini, The Doctrine of Fascism (1932)

- Bonhoeffer, Dietrich. *Life Together, 1939.* Translated by John W. Doberstein. New York: Harper & Row, 1954.

- Booth, Philip. *Catholic Social Teaching and the Market Economy.* London: Institute of Economic Affairs, 2007.

- Bunyan, John. *The Pilgrim's Progress, 1678.* Edited by Roger Sharrock. London: Penguin Classics, 1987.

- Campbell, Joseph. *The Hero with a Thousand Faces, 1949.* Princeton, NJ: Princeton University Press, 1968.

- Clark, Kevin, and Ravi Jain. *The Liberal Arts Tradition: A Philosophy of Christian Classical Education.* Camp Hill, PA: Classical Academic Press, 2019.

- Cooper, Jordan B. *Critique of David Bentley Hart's Interpretations of the New Testament.* Just and Sinner Publications, 2017.

- Cooper, Jordan B. *In Defense of the True, the Good, and the Beautiful: On the Loss of Transcendence and the Decline of the West.* Just and Sinner Publications, 2021.

- Cooper, Jordan B. *The Doctrine of God: A Defense of Classical Christian Theism*. Just and Sinner Publications, 2023.
- Cooper, Jordan B. *Scholastic Method Lectures.* Just and Sinner Publications, 2025.
- Dante Alighieri. *Divine Comedy, 1320*. Translated by John Ciardi. New York: W.W. Norton & Company, 1970.
- Deneen, Patrick J. *Why Liberalism Failed.* New Haven, CT: Yale University Press, 2018.
- Dreher, Rod. *The Benedict Option: A Strategy for Christians in a Post-Christian Nation*. New York: Sentinel, 2017.
- Dugdale, Lydia. *The Lost Art of Dying: Reviving Forgotten Wisdom*. New York: HarperOne, 2021.
- Erasmus of Rotterdam. *The Praise of Folly*. Translated by Clarence H. Miller. 1511. Reprint, New Haven: Yale University Press, 2003.
- Fichte, Johann Gottlieb. *Addresses to the German Nation, 1808*. Translated by R.F. Jones and G.H. Turnbull. Chicago: Open Court Publishing, 1922.
- Gaylord, Whitefield G. *Lutheran Education: From Wittenberg to the Future*. St. Louis, MO: Concordia Publishing House, 2011.
- Gillespie, Michael Allen. *The Theological Origins of Modernity*. Chicago: University of Chicago Press, 2008.
- Grimm, Jacob, and Wilhelm. *Grimm's Fairy Tales, 1812–1857*. Translated by Margaret Hunt. London: George Bell & Sons, 1884.

- Guinness, Os. *Renaissance: The Power of the Gospel However Dark the Times.* Downers Grove, IL: InterVarsity Press, 2014.
- Harran, Marilyn J. *Martin Luther: Learning for Life.* St. Louis, MO: Concordia Publishing House, 1997.
- Herbert, Frank. *Dune.* Philadelphia: Chilton Books, 1965.
- *The Holy Bible, English Standard Version.* Wheaton, IL: Crossway, 2001.
- Homer. *Odyssey, circa 8th century BC.* Translated by Robert Fagles. New York: Penguin Classics, 1996.
- Hooker, Richard. *Of the Laws of Ecclesiastical Polity, 1593–1597.* Edited by Arthur Stephen McGrade. Cambridge: Cambridge University Press, 1989.
- Huxley, Aldous. *Brave New World.* London: Chatto & Windus, 1932.
- Ian Hutchinson, Can a Scientist Believe in Miracles? (2018)
- Iwabuchi, Koichi. *Recentering Globalization: Popular Culture and Japanese Transnationalism.* Durham, NC: Duke University Press, 2002.
- Jay, Martin. *Magical Nominalism. Thesis Eleven*, 2025.
- Jefferson, Thomas. *Letter to Charles Yancey, 1816.* In *The Writings of Thomas Jefferson*, edited by Andrew A. Lipscomb and Albert Ellery Bergh. Washington, DC: Thomas Jefferson Memorial Association, 1905.

- Keller, Timothy. *Hope in Times of Fear: The Resurrection and the Meaning of Easter.* New York: Viking, 2021.
- Kern, Andrew, and Gene Edward Veith. *Classical Education: The Movement Sweeping America.* Washington, DC: Capital Research Center, 2015.
- Kevin J. Vanhoozer, The Drama of Doctrine (2005)
- Lewis, C.S. *An Experiment in Criticism.* Cambridge: Cambridge University Press, 1961.
- Lewis, C.S. *On Stories: And Other Essays on Literature.* Edited by Walter Hooper. New York: Harcourt Brace Jovanovich, 1966.
- Lewis, C.S. *The Abolition of Man.* London: Oxford University Press, 1943.
- Lewis, C.S. *The Chronicles of Narnia, 1950–1956.* London: Geoffrey Bles, 1950–1956.
- Lewis, C.S. *The Screwtape Letters.* London: Geoffrey Bles, 1942.
- Luther, Martin. *To the Councilmen of All Cities in Germany That They Establish and Maintain Christian Schools, 1524.* In *Luther's Works*, Vol. 45, edited by Walther I. Brandt. Philadelphia: Fortress Press, 1962.
- Littlejohn, Bradford. *"Fare Forward": The Influence of Christian Humanism on the Classical Christian Education Movement.* Lynchburg, VA: Liberty University Press, 2020.
- MacArthur, John. *Overcoming Materialism* (sermon). Panorama City, CA: Grace to You, 1980.

- Malory, Thomas. *Le Morte d'Arthur, 1485*. Edited by Stephen H.A. Shepherd. New York: W.W. Norton & Company, 2004.
- Miyazaki, Hayao. *Spirited Away* (film). Tokyo: Studio Ghibli, 2001.
- Montgomery, J. Warwick. *In Defense of Martin Luther*. Milwaukee: Northwestern Publishing House, 1970.
- Montgomery, J. Warwick. *The Suicide of Christian Theology*. Minneapolis: Bethany Fellowship, 1970.
- Moore, Alan. *The Dark Knight Returns*. New York: DC Comics, 1986.
- Moreland, J.P. *Love Your God with All Your Mind: The Role of Reason in the Life of the Soul*. Colorado Springs, CO: NavPress, 1997.
- Newton, John. *Amazing Grace, 1779*. In *Olney Hymns*. London: W. Oliver, 1779.
- Nujabes. *Metaphorical Music* (album). Tokyo: Hydeout Productions, 2003.
- Ockham, William. *Summa Logicae, circa 1323*. Edited by Philotheus Boehner. St. Bonaventure, NY: Franciscan Institute, 1957.
- Origen. *Homilies on Luke, circa 233–244 AD*. Translated by Joseph T. Lienhard. Washington, DC: Catholic University of America Press, 1996.
- Orwell, George. *1984*. London: Secker & Warburg, 1949.

- Plato. *Republic, circa 375 BC.* Translated by G.M.A. Grube, revised by C.D.C. Reeve. Indianapolis: Hackett Publishing, 1992.

- Röpke, Wilhelm. *A Humane Economy: The Social Framework of the Free Market.* Chicago: Henry Regnery Company, 1960.

- Rueter, David L. *Teaching the Faith at Home: What Does This Mean? How Is This Done?*. St. Louis, MO: Concordia Publishing House, 2016.

- Sapkowski, Andrzej. *The Witcher* (book series), 1993–1999. Translated by Danusia Stok and David French. New York: Orbit Books, 2007–2017.

- Schaeffer, Francis. *How Should We Then Live? The Rise and Decline of Western Thought and Culture.* Old Tappan, NJ: Fleming H. Revell, 1976.

- Søren Kierkegaard, Fear and Trembling (1843)

- *Star Wars* (original trilogy, films). Directed by George Lucas. Los Angeles: Lucasfilm, 1977–1983.

- *The Kissing Booth* (film series). Directed by Vince Marcello. Los Angeles: Netflix, 2018–2021.

- *The Lord of the Rings* (film trilogy). Directed by Peter Jackson. Los Angeles: New Line Cinema, 2001–2003.

- *The Matrix.* Directed by the Wachowskis. Los Angeles: Warner Bros., 1999.

- *The Matrix Reloaded* and *The Matrix Revolutions.* Directed by the Wachowskis. Los Angeles: Warner Bros., 2003.

- *The Matrix Resurrections.* Directed by Lana Wachowski. Los Angeles: Warner Bros., 2021.
- *The Rings of Power* (TV series). Los Angeles: Amazon Prime, 2022.
- *The Witcher* (TV series). Los Angeles: Netflix, 2019–present.
- Tolkien, J.R.R. *The Lord of the Rings, 1954–1955.* London: George Allen & Unwin, 1954–1955.
- Uyama Hiroto. *A Son of the Sun* (album). Tokyo: Hydeout Productions, 2008.
- Veith, Gene Edward. *Classical Education: The Movement Sweeping America*. Washington, DC: Capital Research Center, 2015.
- Veith, Gene Edward. *The Spirituality of the Cross: The Way of the First Evangelicals.* St. Louis, MO: Concordia Publishing House, 1999.
- Virgil. *Aeneid, 29–19 BC.* Translated by Robert Fitzgerald. New York: Vintage Classics, 1990.
- Wesley, Charles. *Hark! The Herald Angels Sing, 1739.* In *Hymns and Sacred Poems.* London: Strahan, 1739.
- Wright, N.T. *Surprised by Hope: Rethinking Heaven, the Resurrection, and the Mission of the Church.* New York: HarperOne, 2008, with 2024 reflections.
- *York Mystery Plays, 14th–16th centuries.* Edited by Richard Beadle and Pamela M. King. Oxford: Oxford University Press, 1999.

Reports and Studies

- Association of Classical Christian Schools (ACCS). *Reports on Student Outcomes.* Purcellville, VA: ACCS, 2023.
- Carnegie Endowment for International Peace. *Global Protest Tracker, 2024–2025 Projections.* Washington, DC: Carnegie Endowment, 2025.
- Classical Christian Education Market Projections, 2025.
- Deloitte. *Digital Trends Report, 2025.* New York: Deloitte, 2025.
- Florida Department of Education. *Book Ban Reports, 2023–2024.* Tallahassee, FL: Florida DOE, 2024.
- Japanese Government Surveys. *Hikikomori Estimates, 2023.* Tokyo: Ministry of Health, Labour and Welfare, 2023.
- Lifeway Research. *Global Christianity Trends, 2025.* Nashville, TN: Lifeway Research, 2025.
- National Assessment of Educational Progress (NAEP). *Civics Proficiency Data, 2024.* Washington, DC: U.S. Department of Education, 2024.
- National Assessment of Educational Progress (NAEP). *Reading Proficiency Data, 2024.* Washington, DC: U.S. Department of Education, 2024.
- Pew Research Center. *Gen Z Religious Affiliation and Mental Health, 2025.* Washington, DC: Pew Research Center, 2025.

- Pew Research Center. *Religious Trends Report, 2025.* Washington, DC: Pew Research Center, 2025.
- Pew Research Center. *Teens, Social Media, and Technology, 2022–2025.* Washington, DC: Pew Research Center, 2025.
- United Nations. *Demographic Data on Japan's Birth Rate, 2024*. New York: UN Department of Economic and Social Affairs, 2024.
- U.S. Department of Education. *No Child Left Behind Act, 2001*. Washington, DC: U.S. Government Printing Office, 2001.
- U.S. Government. *Troubled Asset Relief Program (TARP), 2008*. Washington, DC: U.S. Department of the Treasury, 2008.
- U.S. Surgeon General. *Advisory on Loneliness, 2023–2025.* Washington, DC: U.S. Department of Health and Human Services, 2023–2025.
- World Health Organization. *Adolescent Mental Health and Social Media Use, 2018–2022*. Geneva: WHO, 2022.
- World Health Organization. *Global Mental Health Report, 2024*. Geneva: WHO, 2024.

Additional Sources

- *Batman v Superman: Dawn of Justice* and *Justice League* (films). Directed by Zack Snyder. Los Angeles: Warner Bros., 2016–2017.
- *Dune* (film). Directed by Denis Villeneuve. Los Angeles: Warner Bros., 2021.

- *Final Fantasy Tactics* (video game). Tokyo: Square, 1997.
- *Mass Effect* (video game trilogy). Edmonton: BioWare, 2007–2012.
- *Oberammergau Passion Play*. Performed since 1634. Oberammergau, Germany.
- *Star Wars: The Force Awakens* to *The Rise of Skywalker* (films). Directed by J.J. Abrams and Rian Johnson. Los Angeles: Lucasfilm, 2015–2019.
- *Steins; Gate* (visual novel and anime). Tokyo: 5pb. and Nitroplus, 2009–2011.

www.ingramcontent.com/pod-product-compliance
Lightning Source LLC
LaVergne TN
LVHW020719110826
845149LV00012B/2326

* 9 7 8 1 9 6 9 1 7 2 0 9 0 *